# PLAY GAMES WITH ENGLISH 2

## TEACHER'S RESOURCE BOOK

**COLIN GRANGER**
with illustrations by John Plumb

**Revised edition in 3 levels**

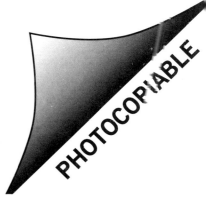

# Heinemann Games Series

**Titles in this series include:**

**Play Games With English Teacher's Resource Book 1** Colin Granger 0 435 25016 7
**Play Games With English Teacher's Resource Book 2** Colin Granger 0 435 25017 5

**Word Games with English 1** Deirdre Howard-Williams & Cynthia Herd 0 435 28380 4
**Word Games with English 2** Deirdre Howard-Williams & Cynthia Herd 0 435 28381 2
**Word Games with English 3** Deirdre Howard-Williams & Cynthia Herd 0 435 28382 0
**Word Games with English Plus** Deirdre Howard-Williams & Cynthia Herd 0 435 28379 0

**English Puzzles 1** Doug Case 0 435 28280 8
**English Puzzles 2** Doug Case 0 435 28281 6
**English Puzzles 3** Doug Case 0 435 28282 4
**English Puzzles 4** Doug Case 0 435 28283 2

Heinemann English Language Teaching
a division of Heinemann Publishers (Oxford) Ltd
Halley Court, Jordan Hill, Oxford OX2 8EJ

OXFORD   MADRID   ATHENS   PARIS   FLORENCE   PRAGUE   SÃO PAULO
CHICAGO   SYDNEY   AUCKLAND   SINGAPORE   TOKYO   GABORONE
JOHANNESBURG   PORTSMOUTH (NH)   IBADAN

ISBN 0 435 25017 5

## Acknowledgements

We would like to thank David King of the Eurocentre in Brighton for his help in the preparation of this book. Also to teachers at the Migros Klubschule, Basle. Finally to Jathan and Nicola for ideas and suggestions for language games.

© Colin Granger and John Plumb 1993
First published 1993

All rights reserved; no part of this publication may be reproduced, stored in a retrieval system, or transmitted in any form or by any means, electronic, mechanical, photocopying, recording, or otherwise, without the prior written permission of the Publishers.

Cover designed by Martin Cox
Illustrations and student's pages designed by John Plumb
Teacher's pages typeset by The Design Syndicate

Printed in and bound in Great Britain by Thomson Litho Ltd, East Kilbride

93 94 95 96 97 10 9 8 7 6 5 4 3 2

# CONTENTS

**TEACHER'S INTRODUCTION** ... 5

## MEMORY 1 ... 6
Present Continuous + Object Pronouns
*A porter is fetching them a screen.*
### Mime Game ... 6
Present Continuous + Object Pronouns
*Are you showing him a book?*

## THE NAME GAME ... 8
Verb to be + This/These + Singular and Plural Nouns
*What's this? It's a cooker. What are these? They're plates.*
### The Name Game extension ... 8
Verb to be + This/These + Singular and Plural Nouns
*What's this? It's a lighter. What are these? They're batteries.*

## SPOT THE DIFFERENCE 1 ... 10
There is/There are + Some/Any + Countable/Uncountable Nouns
*There is some fruit salad. There aren't any chips.*
### Lists Game ... 10
There is/There are + A/Some + Countable/Uncountable Nouns
*There's a lipstick. There are some envelopes.*

## CATEGORIES 1 ... 12
Vocabulary
### Categories 1 extension ... 12
Vocabulary
### Southampton ... 12
Vocabulary
### Last is First ... 12
Vocabulary

## JOBS QUIZ ... 14
Present Simple *Carpenters make things from wood.*
### Detective Story: 'The Lift Mystery' ... 14
Present Simple *Does he walk upstairs because he wants some exercise?*
### Detective Story: 'Mystery Phone-Call' ... 14
Present Simple *Do you know the person who answers the phone?*

## MEMORY 2 ... 16
Numbers *four hundred and two, the fifth floor*
Dates *It's May the sixth.*
Time *It's twelve forty-five.*
### The Number Game ... 16
Numbers *five, fifth*

## SPOT THE DIFFERENCE 2 ... 18
Should be + Prepositions of Place
*The towel should be behind the door.*
### What's Different? ... 18
Should be + Prepositions of Place
*The cassette player should be on my desk.*
### Picture Dictation ... 18
There is/There are + Prepositions of Place
*There's a house in the centre of the picture.*

## SIGNS ... 20
Imperative *Do not lean out of the window.*
### The Instruction Game ... 20
Imperative *Walk to the back of the room.*
### Instruction Follow On ... 20
Imperative *Close your book.*

## OBJECTS QUIZ ... 22
Verb to be + Adjective *It's quite big but it isn't very heavy.*
Present Simple Passive *It is used by photographers.*
### Objects Quiz extension ... 22
Verb to be + Adjective *They are small.*
Present Simple Passive *It is used by photographers.*

## PICTURE STORY ... 24
Past Simple *Frank woke up.*
### Detective Story: 'The Sawdust Mystery' ... 24
Past Simple *Was he murdered? Did he kill himself?*
### Detective Story: 'Suicide! But how?' ... 24
Past Simple

## CONNECTIONS 1 ... 26
Adverbs of Manner *He drives very dangerously.*
### Invention Game ... 26
Adverbs of Manner *I was talking quietly.*
### Charades ... 26
Adverbs of Manner *You're working clumsily.*

## CLOSE-UPS 1 ... 28
Going to Future *She's going to play the piano.*
### Invention Game ... 28
Going to Future *I'm going to go camping. I'm going to take it to the zoo.*

## COMPARATIVE QUIZ ... 30
Comparative *A sea is larger than a lake.*
Superlative *An ocean is the largest.*
### Comparative Quiz extension ... 30
Comparative *City Z is larger than City Y.*
Superlative *City X is the largest.*
### Comparison Game ... 30
Comparative *Magazines are usually more expensive. Magazines are usually thicker.*

## MEMORY 3 ... 32
Present Perfect Simple *She's packed her suitcase. He hasn't packed his suitcase.*
### Long Sentence Game ... 32
Present Perfect Simple *I've washed the dishes.*
### What's Different? ... 32
Present Perfect Simple *You've opened the matchbox.*

## OBSERVATION 1 ... 34
Should *You shouldn't drive you car in the park.*
### Where is it? ... 34
Should *You should hold the handrail.*
Must *You mustn't stand too near the sides.*

## CONNECTIONS 2 ... 36
Infinitive of Purpose *I went to the estate agent's to look for a house.*
### Invention Game ... 36
Infinitive of Purpose *I went to the bank to change some money.*

## MEMORY 4 ... 38
Past Continuous *I was standing at the front of the queue.*
### Private Eye ... 38
Past Continuous *What were you wearing? I was wearing a suit.*
### Detective Story: 'Surprise Thank You' ... 38
Past Continuous *Were they quarrelling?*
Past Simple *Did the barman know the man?*

## BY WHOM? ... 40
Passive-(was done) *'Yesterday' was sung by the Beatles.*
### Famous Places Quiz ... 40
Passive-(was done) *Napoleon was exiled on Elba.*

## SPOT THE DIFFERENCE 3 ... 42
Present Perfect + Yet *He has washed the tea towels. He hasn't done the washing up yet.*
### Invention Game ... 42
Present Perfect *I've read the dialogue.*
### Action Game ... 42
Going to Future *You're going to open the door.*
Present Continuous *You're opening the door.*
Present Perfect + Just *You've just opened the door.*

## MEMORY 5 ... 44
Anybody/Anything/Anywhere *Was there anybody choosing a book? Was there anything written on the blackboard? Was there a clock anywhere in the classroom?*
### Memory 5 extension ... 44
Anybody/Anything/Anywhere *Is there anybody in the room wearing a blue shirt? Is there anything on the floor near the door? Is there an umbrella anywhere in the room?*

## SPELLING QUIZ ... 46
Spelling; Vocabulary; Adjectives; Plural Nouns
### Top and Tails ... 46
Spelling; Vocabulary

## Contents continued...

### CONNECTIONS 3 — 48
Question Tags *Yes, isn't it?*
So/Nor *So do I./Nor can I.*

**Agree or Die** — 48
So/Nor *So do I./Nor can I.*

**Surprise** — 48
Questions Tags *You haven't, have you?*

### OBSERVATION 2 — 50
Present Perfect Continuous *She has been pruning the tree.*

**Sherlock Holmes** — 50
Present Perfect Continuous *Have you been working?*

### MEMORY 6 — 52
Past Continuous *He was listening to the radio.*

**Detective Story: 'Murder in broad daylight'** — 52
Past Continuous *Were the two men walking on the same side of the street?*
Past Simple *Did they know the woman?*

### SPORTS QUIZ — 54
May *Each team may have up to eleven players ...*
Should *One team should wear blue caps ...*
Must *Players must not splash water ...*
Can *The game can be played by two or four players.*

**Sports Quiz extension** — 54
May; Should; Must; Can

### CLOSE-UPS 2 — 56
Could be *It could be a watch.*

**Noises Off** — 56
Could be *It could be a pair of scissors.*

### CATEGORIES 2 — 58
For/Since *for two days/since last night*

**Voting Game** — 58
For/Since *for quite a while/since midnight*

### OBSERVATION 3 — 60
Will (Predictions) *Don't touch that wire. You'll get an electric shock.*

**Help!** — 60
Will (Offers) *I'll answer it.*

### MEMORY 7 — 62
Used to *There used to be a post office.*
*There didn't use to be a supermarket.*

**The Good Old Days** — 62
Used to *They used to salt it.*

### THE WORD ORDER GAME — 64
Word Order; Adverbs of Frequency
*He usually wakes up at half-past seven.*

**The Word Order Game extension** — 64
Word Order; Adverbs of Frequency

**Make a sentence** — 64
Word Order

### OBSERVATION 4 — 66
Present Perfect Continuous *These two children have been swimming.*

**Long Sentence Game** — 66
Present Perfect Continuous *I've been sitting in the garden.*

### DEFINITIONS — 68
Relative Pronoun (Who) + Present Simple
*A journalist is someone who writes for a newspaper.*

**Crossword Puzzles** — 68
Relative Pronouns (Who/Where/That) *Someone who employs people. A place where you live. Something that you tidy your hair with.*

### MEMORY 8 — 70
Lot of/Few/Little + Countable and Uncountable Nouns
*There were a lot of eggs. There were only a few grapes.*
*There was a lot of cheese. There was only a little butter.'*

**Voting Game** — 70
Lot of + Countable and Uncountable Nouns *There were a lot of.chairs. There was a lot of furniture.*

**Long Sentence Game** — 70
Too Many/Too Much + Countable and Uncountable Nouns
*At the party there were too many people and there was too much noise.*

### OPPOSITES QUIZ — 72
Adjectives (Prefixes) *incorrect, uncomfortable, dishonest*

**Voting Game** — 72
Adjectives (Prefixes) *mispronounce, impersonal, indirect*

### WHERE? — 74
First Conditional (If + Will) *If you go to Berlin, you'll see the Brandenburg Gate.*

**Local Knowledge Quiz** — 74
First Conditional (If + Will/Might) *How long will it take if I travel to Brighton by train? Who might you meet if you go to Buckingham Palace?*

### OBSERVATION 5 — 76
Going to Future *A woman is going to dive into the water.*
Present Perfect Simple + Just *A man has just dived into the water.*

**Just Done** — 76
Present Perfect Simple + Just *Have you just had an accident?*

**What's Different?** — 76
Present Perfect Simple + Just *You've just opened a drawer.*

### CATEGORIES 3 — 78
Phrasal Verbs *take off, look after, ring up*

**Storytelling** — 78
Phrasal Verbs *I woke up and put my hand out of bed.*

### BIRTHDAY QUIZ — 80
Second Conditional *I'd wear the cardigan.*

**Imagine Quiz** — 80
Second Conditional *I'd be upset.*

### MEMORY 9 — 82
Present Perfect Simple Passive
*The picture has been taken off the wall.*

**Memory 9 extension** — 82
Present Perfect Simple Passive *The lights have been switched on.*

### VOCABULARY QUIZ — 84
Vocabulary Revision

**ABC Game** — 84
Vocabulary Revision

### MEMORY 1 — 87
### MEMORY 2 — 88
### MEMORY 3 — 89
### MEMORY 4 — 90
### MEMORY 5 — 91
### MEMORY 6 — 92
### MEMORY 7 — 93
### MEMORY 8 — 94
### MEMORY 9 — 95
### INDEX — 96

# TEACHER'S INTRODUCTION

In **Play Games with English 2** you will find **40 main games** on the photocopiable students' pages of the book and a further **55 follow-up games** outlined on the accompanying teacher's pages. Please note that you need to photocopy 2 pages for some of the **Memory** games. On pages where you see a hand with a pen symbol ask the students to write the answers in their exercise books.

**Play Games with English 2** can be used in two ways:

- *systematically* Playing each game in turn with as many of the follow up games as you think necessary. As the games are graded, you will be providing systematic practice of language structures appropriate to students at an elementary level. The **Contents** list on page 3 will show you what language feature each game practises.

- *selectively* Choosing and playing games to provide additional practice of points you feel your students need extra help with. The **Index of Structures and Language Points** on page 96 will help you to select games to fit your students' needs.

## USING LANGUAGE GAMES IN THE CLASSROOM

Most games in **Play Games With English Book 2** are best played in four stages:

1. *The rules of the game*
   Generally, the best way of getting the students to understand how a game is played is not to explain the rules but to play a trial round with the students.

2. *Choosing sides*
   The games in **Play Games With English Book 2** can be played in the following ways:

   • *Player A v. Player B* Here each person in the class plays against each other.
   • *Small team v. Small team* Here the class is divided up into a number of small teams.
   • *Team A v. Team B* Here the class is divided into two teams.
   • *You v. the Class* Here you (or individual students in turn) play against the rest of the class.
   Some games are best played in one particular way; in others you can be more flexible. If the students organise themselves into teams, make sure that not all the best students end up in the same team.

3. *Playing the game*
   In games involving team discussion, stress to your students that the working language should, as far as possible, be English.

   *Correction* While the game is being played, any correction of mistakes should be done in as unobtrusive a way as possible so as not to distract from the game.

4. *Follow up*
   The purpose of this stage is to focus the students' attention on the main language points practised in the game. At this stage, any mistakes made during the game can be corrected and any new vocabulary written up.

# MEMORY 1

**Present Continuous + Object Pronouns:** *A porter is fetching them a screen.*

*Photocopy pages 7 and 87 to play this game.*

Divide the class into small teams of two to three players and appoint team secretaries. Hand out page 7 and give the teams two minutes to study and memorise the picture. Then get the teams to cover or hand you back page 7. Hand out page 87 and go through the example with the class. The team secretaries, helped by the rest of their team, write down what the various people in the hospital ward are doing, using the picture prompts. Make sure they understand that each sentence should include an object pronoun. The team with the most correct sentences is the winner.

| ANSWERS: | 1. A porter is fetching them a screen. |
|---|---|
| | 2. The matron is giving her an injection. |
| | 3. A visitor is bringing her some flowers. |
| | 4. A nurse is passing him a thermometer. |
| | 5. A patient is lending her a pen. |
| | 6. A visitor is pouring him a glass of water. |
| | 7. A doctor is showing them an X-ray. |

## MIME GAME

**Present Continuous + Object Pronouns:** *Are you showing him a book?*

Tell the class that you are going to mime an action which they have to guess. Write the action on a piece of paper: *I'm showing him some holiday photos.* Choose a player to do the mime with and show him or her what is written on the piece of paper. Mime the action for the rest of the class to guess: *Are you showing him a book? Are you showing him a letter?* Get the player you are doing the mime with to answer their questions with *Yes, he/she is* or *No, he/she isn't.* (Your mime does not have to be good – the more amateur the mime, the more questions will have to be asked.) Give verbal hints if necessary and tell the class when they are getting warm. The player who guesses the mime then gets the chance to mime the next action for the others to guess, and so on, till everyone has had a turn.

Example actions: *I'm giving her a tip, I'm passing him the salt. I'm telling them a joke. I'm offering her a light. I'm showing them my passport photo. I'm fetching her a bandage. I'm asking him the way. I'm bringing them a drink.*

**Hints:** Make sure that when the players mime *pass, fetch* and *bring* they show the differences between these verbs.

Look at this picture of a busy hospital ward. Try to remember what everyone is doing.

You have two minutes.

# THE NAME GAME

**Verb *to be*:** *What's this? It's a cooker.*
***This/These*** *What are these? They're plates.*
**Singular and Plural Nouns**

Divide the class into small teams of two to three players and appoint team secretaries. The team secretaries, helped by the rest of their team, write down all the things they can identify in English. Set a five minute time limit for them to complete this task. At the end, the team with the most correct answers is the winner.

**Hints:** Practice *What's this?/What are these?* questions afterwards by getting students to ask and answer about the objects in the picture.

| ANSWERS: | | | | |
|---|---|---|---|---|
| | 1. | It's a cooker. | 10. | They're spoons. |
| | 2. | They're plates. | 11. | They're saucepans. |
| | 3. | It's a dishwasher. | 12. | It's a sink. |
| | 4. | They're forks. | 13. | They're mugs. |
| | 5. | It's a washing machine. | 14. | They're cups. |
| | 6. | They're knives. | 15. | It's a tray. |
| | 7. | It's a toaster. | 16. | They're scissors. |
| | 8. | It's an iron. | 17. | They're bowls. |
| | 9. | It's a microwave oven. | 18. | It's a frying pan. |

## *THE NAME GAME – extension*

**Verb *to be*:** *What's this? It's a lighter.*
***This/These*:** *What are these? They're batteries.*
**Singular and Plural Nouns**

Working in small teams of two or three players, get the students to put together a collection of ten objects made up of their personal possessions, e.g. *a lighter, two batteries, a hair slide, two safety pins, a penknife, two combs, a business card, two cassettes, a pencil sharpener, a watch strap*. While they are doing this, go round the class and check that there is not too much duplication of objects and that the things chosen are neither too obscure nor too easy. The students then have to write a list of their objects in English. If necessary, they could use dictionaries to help them do this or ask you. Each team then challenges the class to name their objects. They should do this by holding up each object in turn and asking *What's this?* or *What are these?* The teams should write their answers down *(It's/They're ...)* after consultation with their fellow team members. Award team totals (1 point per correct answer) after each round.

**Hints:** This game could be made easier by getting the teams to give the initial letter(s) of the object when they ask their questions, e.g. *What's this? It begins with an L. What are these? They begin with a B.*

# THE NAME GAME

## How many things can you name?

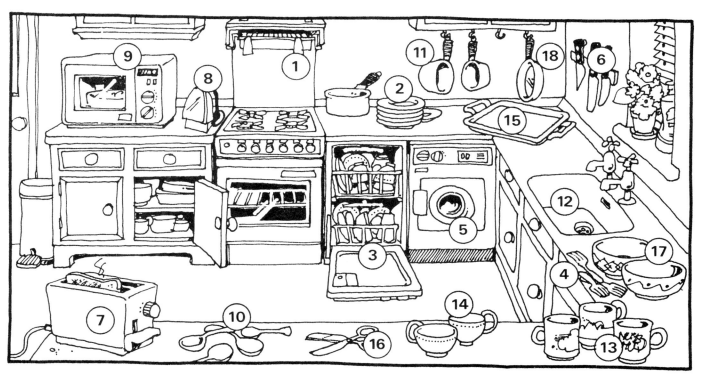

1. It's a cooker.
2. They're plates.
3. ..................................................
4. ..................................................
5. ..................................................
6. ..................................................
7. ..................................................
8. ..................................................
9. ..................................................
10. ..................................................
11. ..................................................
12. ..................................................
13. ..................................................
14. ..................................................
15. ..................................................
16. ..................................................
17. ..................................................
18. ..................................................

© Colin Granger and John Plumb 1993

## SPOT THE DIFFERENCE 1

***There is/There are + Some/Any + Countable/Uncountable Nouns:*** *There is some fruit salad. There aren't any chips.*

Working individually or in pairs, the players write down the differences between picture A and picture B. Set a five-minute time limit. The player with the most correct sentences is the winner.

| ANSWERS: | There is some orange juice. | There isn't any steak. |
| | There is a chocolate cake. | There isn't any apple pie. |
| | There are some sausage rolls. | There aren't any chicken sandwiches. |

## LISTS GAME

***There is/There are + A/Some + Countable/Uncountable Nouns:*** *There's a lipstick. There are some envelopes.*

Divide the class into two teams and appoint team secretaries. Ask each team to prepare a collection of objects on a table or desk. They should use personal possessions to make up these collections which should consist of twenty objects in all. Make sure that some uncountable nouns are included, e.g. *paper, sellotape, string*. The two teams then have one minute to study the other team's collection of objects. The two collections should then be covered while the team secretaries write, with the help of the rest of their team, what the other team's collection comprises of:

*There's a lipstick.*
*There are some envelopes.*
*There's some paper.*
*etc.*

The team secretaries then read out their lists. Score 2 points for each correct observation expressed in correct English, but only 1 point if the English is incorrect. The team with the most points is the winner.

# Spot the Difference 1

Compare the pictures.
What is different in picture B?

There are eight differences.
Try to find them.
Use these forms in your answers:

There is some... a/an...     There are some...     There isn't any...     There aren't any...

In picture B...

1. There is some fruit salad.
2. There aren't any chips.
3. 
4. 
5. 
6. 
7. 
8.

# CATEGORIES 1                                              Vocabulary

Working individually or in pairs, the players write the words under the appropriate category. The first player to do this correctly is the winner.

| ANSWERS: | | |
|---|---|---|
| | **Food:** | rice, spinach, lamb, plums, mushrooms. |
| | **Clothes:** | scarf, suit, vest, coat, jacket. |
| | **Parts of the body:** | stomach, neck, feet, back, arm. |
| | **Transport:** | van, ship, scooter, coach, bicycle. |
| | **Places:** | forest, hill, valley, field, beach. |
| | **Furniture:** | settee, bed, desk, cupboard, wardrobe. |

## CATEGORIES 1 – extension                                 Vocabulary

With the help of the class choose six categories, e.g. *colours, games/sports, animals, fruit/vegetables, jobs, materials*. Each player in turn chooses a letter of the alphabet. All the players then try to find and write down as many words as they can for each of the six categories beginning with the chosen letter. For example, if the chosen letter is *p*, a player might write down:

| Colours | Games/Sports | Animals | Fruit/Vegetables | Jobs | Materials |
|---|---|---|---|---|---|
| pink | polo | pig | plum | painter | plastic |
| | | panda | pineapple | | |
| | | penguin | potato | | |

Set a three-minute time limit. Each player then reads out his or her list of words. If a player has found a word not thought of by any of the other players, he scores 2 points. If, however, one or more of the other players has also thought of the same word, then they all score 1 point. The next player then begins the next round by choosing a different letter, and so on. The player with the highest total of points at the end of the final round is the winner.

## SOUTHAMPTON                                              Vocabulary

Write up the word *Southampton*. Demonstrate how many words the word *Southampton* contains: *so, out, south, ham, am, amp, ton, on*. Write up another long word the class knows, e.g. *information*. Then working individually or in pairs the players write down as many words as they can find in the given word. The words must be of two letters or more. Set a two-minute time limit. The player with the most words is the winner. Continue with other long words.

## LAST IS FIRST                                            Vocabulary

Choose a category in which the class knows a lot of words, e.g. *animals*. The first player calls out a word in that category. The next player then continues with another word in the category beginning with the last letter of the previous word, and so on, for example:

| | |
|---|---|
| Player 1: | *Shee**p**.* |
| Player 2: | *Pi**g**.* |
| Player 3: | *Giraff**e**.* |
| Player 4: | *Elephant.* |

Players get minus points if they *(a)* are unable to think of a word in the category beginning with the last letter of the previous word; *(b)* repeat a word which has been previously used; or *(c)* hesitate too long. The player with the least number of minus points at the end of the game is the winner.

**Hints:** Play a trial round first. You could introduce the rule that whenever a player loses a point, the next player can begin with a new category. The category should be one in which the class knows a lot of words.

# CATEGORIES 1

Put these words in the correct category.

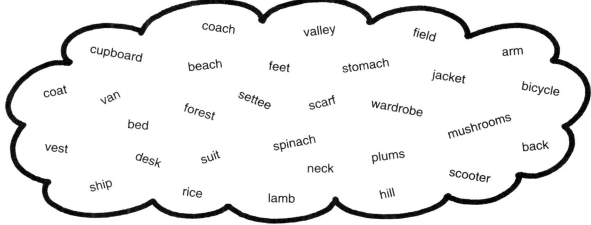

coach, valley, field, cupboard, beach, feet, stomach, arm, jacket, coat, van, scarf, wardrobe, bicycle, settee, bed, forest, mushrooms, vest, spinach, back, desk, suit, plums, neck, scooter, ship, rice, lamb, hill

**FOOD**

rice

**CLOTHES**

**PARTS OF THE BODY**

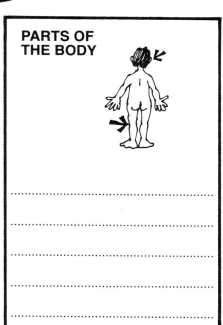

**TRANSPORT**

**PLACES**

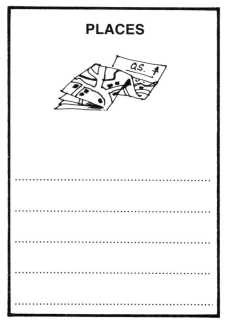

**FURNITURE**

© Colin Granger and John Plumb 1993

# JOBS QUIZ

**Present Simple:** *Carpenters make things from wood.*

Divide the class into two teams, A and B. Team A asks Team B the first question *What do carpenters do?* Team B can consult together before answering *Carpenters make things from wood.* Then Team B asks Team A the second question, and so on, with the rest of the quiz. Score 1 point for each correct answer. At the end, the team with the most points is the winner.

**Hints:** You could extend this quiz by getting the two teams to think of further questions to ask the other team. For example:
*What does a lifeguard do? What does a lumberjack use for his work?*
*Where does a biologist work? What does a car mechanic wear for his work?*
*Does a scaffolder work inside or outside?*

ANSWERS:
1. Carpenters make things from wood.
2. Dockers load and unload ships.
3. Tailors make clothes.
4. A car mechanic uses a spanner.
5. An electrician uses a screwdriver.
6. An accountant uses a calculator.
7. A dressmaker uses a sewing machine.
8. A gardener uses a spade.
9. A decorator uses a brush.
10. A chambermaid works in a hotel.
11. A typist works in an office.
12. A lecturer works in a university.
13. An actor works in a theatre.
14. A sales assistant works in a shop.
15. A machinist works in a factory.
16. 5. (a postman, a bricklayer, a gardener, a farmer, traffic police)
17. A chef.
18. A soldier.
19. A miner.
20. A police officer.
21. A surgeon.
22. An air hostess.

## DETECTIVE STORY: 'THE LIFT MYSTERY'

**Present Simple:** *Does he walk upstairs because he wants some exercise?*

Read the story to the class, explaining any difficult vocabulary. Explain that the class must play detectives and find the solution to the problem.

**The story**
*Bernard lives on the twenty-second floor of a huge block of flats. Every morning he leaves his flat, gets into the lift, travels to the ground floor and goes to work. In the evening he comes home, gets into the lift on the ground floor, travels to the fourteenth floor, gets out of the lift and walks up the stairs to his flat on the twenty-second floor. He does this every evening. Why?*

The class then asks you questions to find the solution to the story. They can only ask questions which have *Yes/No* answers, e.g. *Does he walk upstairs because he wants some exercise? Does he know somebody on the fourteenth floor?* If necessary, give hints to elicit questions, e.g. *Ask questions about what is inside the lift. Ask questions about what Bernard looks like.*

**The solution**
*Bernard is very short and cannot reach the twenty-second button on the lift's control panel. In the morning this doesn't matter as Bernard can easily press the bottom button on the panel for the ground floor, but in the evening he can only reach the button for the fourteenth floor, and so has to walk up the stairs to the twenty-second floor.*

## DETECTIVE STORY: 'MYSTERY PHONE-CALL'

**Present Simple:** *Do you know the person who answers the phone?*

Presentation as for 'The Lift Mystery'.

**The story**
*Every night at about twelve o'clock I get out of bed, go into the next room, pick up the telephone, dial a number and wait. Someone answers the phone and says 'all right'. I put down my receiver, go back into the bedroom, get into bed and go to sleep. I do this every night. Why?*

**The solution**
*The person who answers the phone lives in the next flat to mine. His bedroom is next to mine and the walls are very thin. He has an incredibly loud snore and I telephone him every night in order to wake him up sufficiently to give me time to get to sleep before he starts snoring again.*

# JOBS QUIZ

**What do these people do?**

Put a ✓ in the correct box.

1. **Carpenters**
   - clean cars. ☐
   - make things from wood. ☐
   - lay carpets. ☐

2. **Dockers**
   - build ships. ☐
   - help in hospitals. ☐
   - load and unload ships. ☐

3. **Tailors**
   - make clothes. ☐
   - look after animals. ☐
   - drive large lorries. ☐

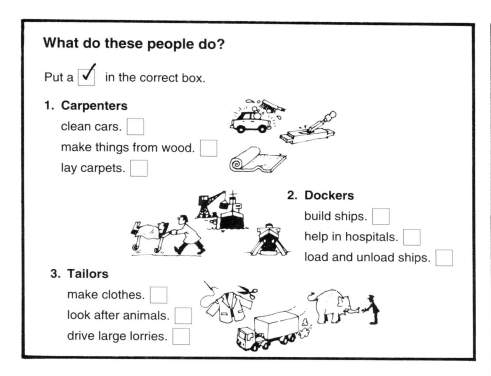

**What do they use for their work?**

4. A car mechanic uses a spanner.

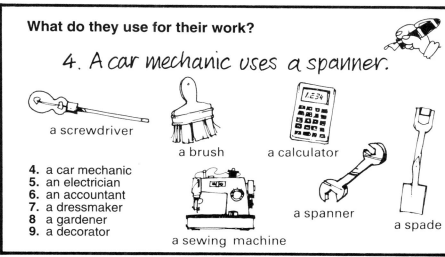

- a screwdriver
- a brush
- a calculator
- a spanner
- a spade
- a sewing machine

4. a car mechanic
5. an electrician
6. an accountant
7. a dressmaker
8. a gardener
9. a decorator

**Where do these people work?**

10. A chambermaid works in a hotel.

10. a chambermaid
11. a typist
12. a lecturer
13. an actor
14. a sales assistant
15. a machinist

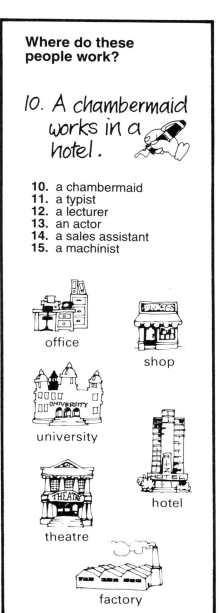

- office
- shop
- university
- hotel
- theatre
- factory

**How many of these people normally work outside in their work?**

16. Write the number in this box. ☐

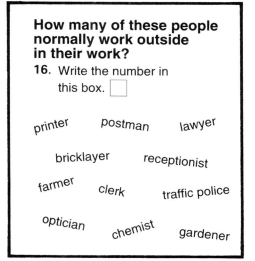

printer   postman   lawyer
bricklayer   receptionist
farmer   clerk   traffic police
optician   chemist   gardener

**Who wears what for their work?**

17. A chef.

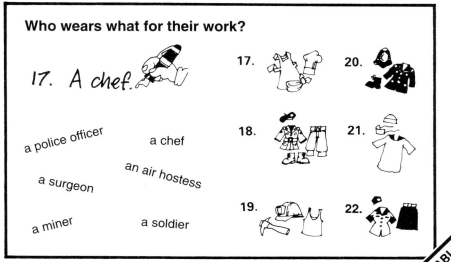

a police officer   a chef
a surgeon   an air hostess
a miner   a soldier

© Colin Granger and John Plumb 1993

# MEMORY 2

**Numbers:** *four hundred and two, the fifth floor*
**Dates:** *It's May the sixth*
**Time:** *It's twelve forty-five*

***Photocopy pages 17 and 88 to play this game.***

Divide the class into small teams of two to three players and appoint team secretaries. Hand out page 17 and give the teams two minutes to study and memorise the picture. Then get the teams to cover or hand you back page 17. Hand out page 88 and go through the example with the class. The team secretaries, helped by the rest of their team, choose the answers to the questions on page 88. They must not look back at the first page while doing this. The team with the most correct answers is the winner.

| ANSWERS: | 1. four hundred and two |
|---|---|
| | 2. seven |
| | 3. the fifth floor |
| | 4. twelve forty-five |
| | 5. May the sixth |
| | 6. one hundred and ten |
| | 7. half past ten |
| | 8. twenty-five pounds |
| | 9. seventeen |

## THE NUMBER GAME

**Numbers:** *five, fifth*

Write up the number 5 at the same time pointing to the first player. This player then has to say what the number is without hesitation. Quickly change 5 to 5th by adding a *th* and point to the second player who has to say *fifth*. The game continues in this way, like a chain drill around the class, with you writing up a new number for each player. Explain that each player has two lives (or three for small class) and write up a 2 for each player as though you were writing up a class plan with students' names. For example:

$$\begin{array}{ccc} & 22 & \\ & 22 & 22 \\ 22 & & 22 \end{array}$$

Change the plan whenever a player loses a life, i.e. $2^1$. Players lose a life if they *(a)* are unable to say (or badly mispronounce) the number you write up; or *(b)* hesitate too long.
Example round:

| | | |
|---|---|---|
| Write *5* on the blackboard. | Player 1: | *Five.* |
| Add a *th*. | Player 2: | *Fifth.* |
| Add another *5* to the left of the first. | Player 3: | *Fifty-fifth.* |
| rub out the *th*. | Player 4: | ... |
| | | (This player hesitates too long and so loses a life.) |
| Add a *5*. | Player 5: | *Five hundred and fifty-five.* |
| Rub out and write up *100*. | Player 6: | *A hundred.* |

And so on, with everybody, apart from Player 4, still with two lives. The last player left in is the winner.
**Hints:** Play a trial round first.
 THE NUMBER GAME should be played at speed.
 Don't forget to practise ordinal as well as cardinal numbers.
 Involve players who are out in refereeing the game.

Look at this picture of a hotel reception. Concentrate on any numbers you see.

You have two minutes.

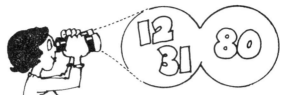

# SPOT THE DIFFERENCE 2

*Should be* + **Prepositions of Place:** *The towel should be behind the door.*

Working individually or in pairs, the players write down the differences between picture A and picture B. Set a ten-minute time limit. The player with the most correct sentences is the winner.

**Hints:** After the players have completed the game you could ask them where the out of place objects are in picture B. For example: *The alarm clock is on the table. The mat is in the middle of the room.*

| ANSWERS: | The towel should be behind the door. |
|---|---|
| | The telephone book should be behind the telephone. |
| | The mat should be in front of the door. |
| | The magazine should be under the table. |
| | The biscuits should be in the tin. |
| | The exercise book should be between the dictionaries. |
| | The cassette-player should be next to the radio. |
| | The alarm clock should be on the shelf. |
| | The saucepan should be on top of the cupboard. |

## WHAT'S DIFFERENT?

*Should be* + **Prepositions of Place:** *The cassette player should be on my desk.*

Leave the room for a short time, telling the class to move an object from its normal position to a new position while you are gone. Come back into the room and try to spot what has been moved, e.g. *The cassette player should be on my desk.* Then individual players can take over the guessing role by leaving the room for a moment while you and the group alter the position of different objects. To score you can either *(a)* time how long each player takes to find which object has been moved and say where it should be in the room (the player with the shortest time being the winner); or *(b)* give a player a minus point if they are unable to see what has been moved or cannot say where the object is normally placed (the player with the least number of minus points at the end of the game is the winner).

## PICTURE DICTATION

*There is/There are* + **Prepositions of Place:** *There's a house in the centre of the picture.*

Explain to the class that they all have to draw a picture which corresponds to a verbal description you are going to dictate to them. Emphasise that the only important thing to get right is the relative positions of the various objects and people you tell them to draw; it is not important how well they are drawn. Begin to dictate the picture giving the players time after each sentence to draw what you have said:

*There's a house in the centre of the picture.*
*There are four windows at the front of the house, two on the ground floor and two on the first.*
*A woman is looking out of the top left-hand window.*
*There's a road in front of the house.*
*There's a bus coming along the road.*
*There's a bus stop just ahead of the bus.*
*A man is waiting at the bus stop.*
*A car is parked opposite the bus stop.*
*There's a woman getting out of the car.*
*There's a railway bridge over the road.*
*A lorry is going under the bridge.*
*There are some trees behind the house.*
*A bird is flying above the trees.*
*There are some clouds in the sky.*
*You can see the sun shining through the clouds.*

Then get the class to compare their pictures. Ask them to make a group decision on who has drawn the most accurate picture. Write up the sentences you have dictated to help them decide. To do this get the players to dictate the sentences back to you using their drawings to remind them of what you said.

# Spot the Difference 2

Nick is very fussy about his things – he likes everything to be in the right place. In picture A everything is where it should be, in picture B some things have been moved. Where should they be?

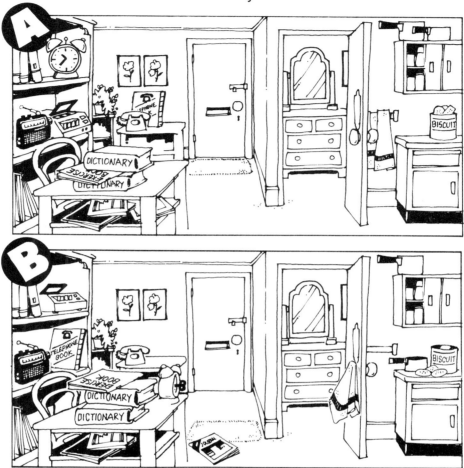

There are nine objects not in the right place. Try to find them.

| Use these prepositions: | | | | | | | |
|---|---|---|---|---|---|---|---|
| behind | in front of | under | in | between | next to | on | on top of |

In picture B...

*The towel should be behind the door.*

# SIGNS

**Imperative:** *Do not lean out of the window.*

Working individually or in pairs, the players write down where the different signs can be seen. The player with the most correct answers is the winner.

**Hints:** Make sure that the class understands what all the signs mean by asking what each one tells us to do or not to do. You could extend this game by writing up other signs for the class to suggest where they might be seen, e.g. *Private — Keep out; Stop; Please knock; Open on the other side; Trespassers will be prosecuted; Shoplifters will be prosecuted; Wait.*

| ANSWERS: | on a bus stop –G | in a zoo – F | in a hospital – I |
|---|---|---|---|
| | in or on a taxi – L | in a park – C | on a railway station platform – A |
| | on an escalator – D | on a door – J | in a street – E |
| | on a gate – H | in a train –B | on a plane – K |

## THE INSTRUCTION GAME

**Imperative:** *Walk to the back of the room.*

Ask a player to leave the room for a moment then, with the help of the rest of the class, hide a book or pen belonging to this player. Ask the player to come back in and guide him to where his missing possession is by using instructions, e.g. *Walk to the back of the room. Look under the table there. Take out the bag. Open the bag and look inside. Take out a small blue pencil case. Open the case. Take out your pen.* Divide the class into two teams, A and B. A player from Team A leaves the room while Team B hides the pen. The player then comes back in and his team has to guide him to the pen as quickly and efficiently as possible by using instructions. The player is only allowed to do what his team tells him to do. Incorrectly expressed instructions must be corrected before the search is allowed to proceed. Time how long it takes to find the pen. A player from Team B then leaves the room while Team A hides the pen, and so on. At the end, the team with the shortest total time is the winner.

## INSTRUCTION FOLLOW ON

**Imperative:** *Close your book.*

Ask the first player to give an instruction to the second player (the instruction must be something the second player can do seated in his or her place). The second player carries out this instruction, tells the third player to do what the first player said and adds a further instruction of his or her own. For example:

> Player 1: *Close your book.*
> (Player 2 closes his book.)
> Player 2: *Close your book and pick up your pen.*
> (Player 3 does these two actions.)
> Player 3: *Close your book. Pick up your pen and take the top off.*
> (Player 4 does these three actions.)

The game continues in this way, like a chain drill around the class. Players lose a point if they *(a)* make a memory mistake in repeating the instructions (i.e. leave out an instruction or get the sequence wrong); *(b)* are unable to think of a new instruction for the next player; *(c)* make a mistake in acting the instructions out (i.e. leave out an instruction or get the sequence wrong); or *(d)* hesitate too long. When a player loses a point the next player continues the game by giving a new instruction to the next player. Example round:

> Player 1: *Close your book.*
> (Player 2 closes his book.)
> Player 2: *Close your book and pick up your pen.*
> (Player 3 does these two actions.)
> Player 3: *Close your book. Pick up your pen and take the top off.*
> Player 4: (This player makes a mistake by acting out the instructions by omitting to close his book and so loses a point.)
> Player 5: (Beginning a new round.) *Turn to page 20.*
> (Player 1 does this.)
> Player 6: *Turn to page 20 but don't look at the page.*
> (Player 2 does this.)

And so on. The player with the least number of minus points at the end of the game is the winner.
**Hints:** Play a trial round first.

Where can you see these signs? Write the letter next to the correct place:

 on a bus stop  G

**A** Passengers Must Not Cross The Line

**B** DO NOT LEAN OUT OF THE WINDOW

**C** DO NOT WALK ON THE GRASS

**D** Please stand on the right

**E** NO PARKING

**F** Please Don't Feed The Animals

**G** QUEUE THIS SIDE

**H** Beware of the dog

**I** NO VISITORS AFTER 9 p.m.

**J** PUSH PULL

**K** FASTEN SEAT BELTS

**L**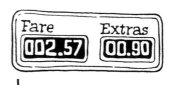

---

 on a bus stop ☐

🚕 in or on a taxi ☐

on an escalator ☐

on a gate ☐

in a zoo ☐

in a park ☐

on a door ☐

in a train ☐

in a hospital ☐

on a railway station platform ☐

in a street ☐

on a plane ☐

© Colin Granger and John Plumb 1993

# OBJECTS QUIZ

**Verb *to be* + Adjectives:** *It's quite big, but it isn't very heavy.*
**Present Simple Passive:** *It is used by photographers. It is made of metal and plastic.*
**Present Simple:** *It has three legs.*

Divide the class into small teams of two to three players and appoint team secretaries. Set a five-minute time limit for the team secretaries, helped by the rest of their team, to complete the task. The team with the most correct answers is the winner.

| ANSWERS: | 1D | 2G | 3C | 4F | 5I | 6A | 7E | 8H | 9B |

## OBJECTS QUIZ – extension

**Verb *to be* + Adjectives:** *They are small.*
**Present Simple Passive:** *They are used to open doors. They are made of metal.*
**Present Simple:** *Nearly everyone uses them.*

Working in small teams of two to three players, get the students to write three descriptions of everyday objects. As they do this, go round the class checking *(a)* that there is not too much duplication of objects between the teams; *(b)* that the descriptions are correctly expressed; *(c)* that the objects are not too easy to guess. The teams then take it in turn to read out their descriptions and challenge the other teams to guess what their objects are. The teams should write their answers down after consultation with their fellow team members. Award points (1 point per correct answer) and work out team totals after each round.

**Hints:** If nobody can guess what the object is, encourage the team which is reading out the description to supply further clues, e.g., *They are very important. People have a big problem if they lose them. Some people attach them to their belts.*

# OBJECTS QUIZ

Match the descriptions to the correct pictures.

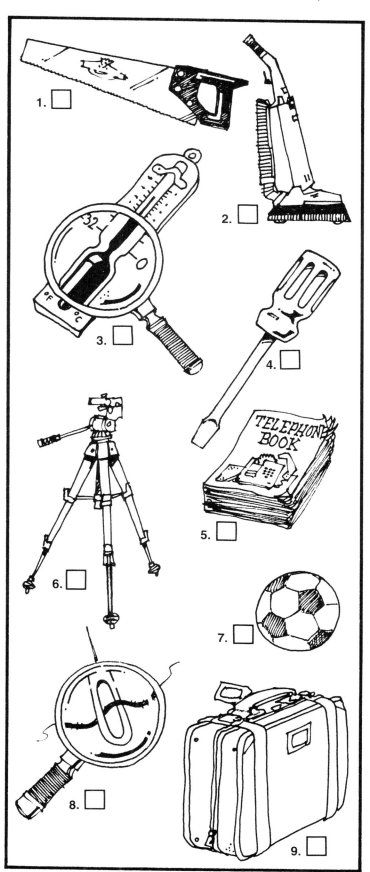

A  It's quite big, but it isn't very heavy. It's made of metal and plastic. It's used by photographers. It has three legs.

B  It has a handle. It's big and rectangular. It's used to transport clothes. It's made of leather and plastic.

C  It's an instrument. It's quite long and thin. It's made of glass, mercury and steel. Doctors and nurses use it for measuring their patients' temperatures.

D  It's a tool. It's used by carpenters to cut wood. It has a handle and a blade. The handle is made of wood or plastic and the blade is made of steel.

E  It's quite big and round. It's made of leather or plastic. It's quite light. It's used to play sport.

F  It's a tool. It's long and thin. It's made of metal and it has a wooden or plastic handle. It's used for turning screws.

G  It's a household appliance. It's quite big. People use it for cleaning carpets. It's made of metal and plastic. It needs electricity to work.

H  It's very small and thin. It's made of steel. It has a pointed end and a very small hole at the top. It's used to sew things.

I  It's square-shaped and very thick. It has many pages. It's made of paper. People use it to find numbers.

© Colin Granger and John Plumb 1993

## PICTURE STORY

**Past Simple:** *Frank woke up.*

Divide the class into small teams of two to three players and appoint team secretaries. The team secretaries, helped by the rest of their team, have to write down what happened to Frank. The team to do this in the shortest time is the winner.

| ANSWERS: | Frank woke up. (c) He heard a noise. (i) He switched on the light. (a) He got out of bed. (o) He put on his dressing gown. (j) He opened the bedroom door. (h) He went downstairs. (m) He listened at the door. (n) He opened the door. (f) He saw a cat outside the window. (g) He went upstairs. (b) He took off his dressing gown. (e) He got into bed. (d) He switched off the light. (k) He went to sleep. (l) |
|---|---|

### DETECTIVE STORY: THE SAWDUST MYSTERY

**Past Simple:** *Was he murdered? Did he kill himself?*

Write up these clues:

**The story**
> A man is lying dead on his bed.
> On the floor is a stick and some sawdust.
> Another man opens the door, looks in, smiles and goes away.

Make sure the the class understand all the clues. Explain that they must play detectives and find the solution to the mystery. The class then asks you questions to try to find the solution to the problem. They can only ask questions which have Yes/No answers, e.g. *Was he murdered? Did he kill himself?* Give hints to elicit questions, e.g.

> Ask questions about how the man died.
> Ask questions about the stick. What it was used for. It's size.
> Ask questions about the sawdust. Where it came from.
> Who produced it.
> Ask questions about where the dead man worked.
> Ask questions about the other man.

**The solution**
> The dead man was the smallest circus midget in the world. He is lying in his caravan. He was blind and because he could not see he had the habit of measuring himself every morning with a special stick (exactly his own size) to make sure that he had not grown in the night. The other man was the second smallest circus midget in the world. He was very jealous of the dead man for being the smallest and, although he didn't personally know the dead midget (he worked for a different circus), he learnt of the measuring habit, crept into the caravan, sawed the stick in half and took away one piece. The smallest circus midget in the world woke up in the morning, felt for his stick and measured himself. To his horror he found he had grown in the night, thought he was no longer the smallest and shot himself. The other man came to the caravan, opened the door, smiled to see his trick had worked and went away — now the smallest midget in the world.

### DETECTIVE STORY: 'SUICIDE! BUT HOW?'

**Past Simple**

Presentation as for THE SAWDUST MYSTERY.

**The story**
> The police broke into a room and found a man hanging from the very high ceiling. The room was completely empty except for a pool of water. The room had been locked from inside. There was no window. It was obviously suicide but how?

**The solution**
> The man had built a platform of ice blocks. The ice melted.

# PICTURE STORY

Put these pictures into the correct order and write the story.

Begin like this:
Last night... Frank woke up. (c) He heard a noise. (i)

# CONNECTIONS 1

**Adverbs of Manner:** *He drives very dangerously.*

Working individually (or in pairs), the players write sentences for each picture. The player who does this in the shortest time is the winner.

| ANSWERS: | | |
|---|---|---|
| | 1. He drives very dangerously. | 6. She sleeps very soundly. |
| | 2. They speak very fluently. | 7. She sings very badly. |
| | 3. He shouts very loudly. | 8. He draws very accurately. |
| | 4. She works very hard. | 9. They play very well. |
| | 5. They run very fast. | |

## INVENTION GAME

**Adverbs of Manner:** *I was talking quietly.*

Divide the class into small teams of two to three players and appoint team secretaries. Write up the basic structure *I was talking ...* Explain that the teams have to write as many sentences as they can using the basic sentence plus an adverb of manner. The sentences must be plausible. For example, the teams could write: *I was talking ... quietly, fluently, slowly, loudly, softly, well, badly, quickly*. Set a five-minute time limit. Then get the teams to read out their sentences in turn. As the other teams read out their answers, the team secretaries should cross out any sentences on their list which are the same. At the end, the team with the most sentences left is the winner. (Check that all the sentences are appropriate.) You could play further games with different basic structures, for example:

*She paints ...*
*He drove ...*

## CHARADES

**Adverbs of Manner:** *You're working clumsily.*

Ask somebody in the class to write an adverb of manner on a slip of paper and hand it to you without anybody else seeing it. Mime the adverb, linking it to an appropriate verb. The rest of the class has to guess what you are miming. For example, you are given the adverb *clumsily* to mime. You decide to mime *working clumsily*. The class asks *Are you ... ing ...ly* questions. Answer by nodding or shaking your head. Write another adverb of manner for a player to mime, for example: *sweetly*. And so on with other adverbs of manner.

# CONNECTIONS 1

Match each picture with one of the adverbs below and write a sentence.

1. drive
2. speak
3. shout
4. work
5. run
6. sleep
7. sing
8. draw
9. play

Use these adverbs:
hard   soundly   badly   fluently   fast   well   accurately   loudly   dangerously

1. He drives very dangerously.
2. 
3. 
4. 
5. 
6. 
7. 
8. 
9. 

© Colin Granger and John Plumb 1993

# CLOSE-UPS 1

**Going to Future:** *She's going to play the piano.*

Working individually or in pairs, the players write down what the woman is going to do in each picture. The first player to do this correctly is the winner.

| ANSWERS: | 1. She's going to play the piano. | 5. She's going to sew on a button. |
|---|---|---|
| | 2. She's going to switch on a radio. | 6. She's going to pick up a coin. |
| | 3. She's going to open a tin. | 7. She's going to stick on a stamp. |
| | 4. She's going to dial a telephone number. | 8. She's going to do up a zip. |

## INVENTION GAME

**Going to Future:** *I'm going to go camping.*
*I'm going to take it to the zoo.*

You need a bag to play this game. Tell the class that they have to pass the bag around from player to player. The player who receives the bag has to look in it, invent an object which could be in the bag and ask the player who has just passed him the bag. *Why have you got a ... in your bag?* This player then has to think of an appropriate reply with *I'm going to*. For example:

| Player 1: | (passes the bag to Player 2) |
| Player 2: | (looks in the bag) |
| | Why have you got a tent in your bag? |
| Player 1: | I'm going to go camping. |

Player 2 then passes the bag to Player 3, and so on, around the class. Emphasise that the players should try to think of an unusual, bizarre object with the intention of making it difficult for the other players to think of a reason for having such an object in their bag. Players get a minus point if they *(a)* can't think of an appropriate reason for having the object in the bag (general formulas such as *I'm going to sell it* or *I'm going to throw it away* are not allowed; or *(b)* hesitate too long. Example round:

| Player 1: | (passes the bag to Player 2) |
| Player 2: | (looks in the bag) |
| | Why have you got a tent in your bag? |
| Player 1: | I'm going to go camping. |
| Player 2: | (passes the bag to Player 3) |
| Player 3: | (looks in the bag) |
| | Why have you got a snake in your bag? |
| Player 2: | I'm going to take it to the zoo. |
| Player 3: | (passes the bag to Player 4) |
| Player 4: | Why have you got some grass in your bag? |
| Player 3: | I'm going to feed my horse. |
| Player 4: | (passes the bag to Player 5) |
| Player 5: | Why have you got a bomb in your bag? |
| Player 4: | (This player can't think of an appropriate reason for having a bomb in his bag and so gets a minus point.) |
| Player 5: | (passes the bag to Player 6) |
| Player 6: | Why have you got a recorder in your bag? |
| Player 5: | I'm going to play it. |

And so on. The player with the least number of minus points at the end of the game is the winner.

**Hints:** Play a trial round first. Give everybody a second chance to think of an appropriate *I'm going to* sentence if the first one is not acceptable.

# CLOSE-UPS 1

Can you tell what she is going to do?

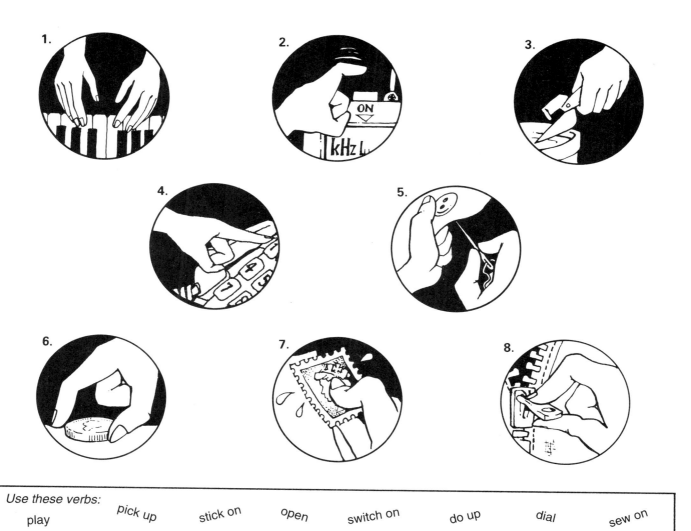

| Use these verbs: | | | | | | | |
|---|---|---|---|---|---|---|---|
| play | pick up | stick on | open | switch on | do up | dial | sew on |

1. She's going to play the piano.
2. 
3. 
4. 
5. 
6. 
7. 
8. 

© Colin Granger and John Plumb 1993

PHOTOCOPIABLE

# COMPARATIVE QUIZ

**Comparative:** *A sea is larger than a lake.*
**Superlative:** *An ocean is the largest.*

Divide the class into small teams of two to three players and appoint team secretaries. The team secretaries, helped by the rest of their team, then complete the quiz. The first team to do this correctly is the winner.

| ANSWERS: | | |
|---|---|---|
| | 1. | Ocean, sea, lake. An ocean is the largest. A sea is larger than a lake. |
| | 2. | Major, captain, sergeant. A major is the most important. A captain is more important than a sergeant. |
| | 3. | City, town, village. A city is the biggest. A town is bigger than a village. |
| | 4. | Whisky, wine, beer. Whisky is the strongest. Wine is stronger than beer. |
| | 5. | Platinum, gold, silver. Platinum is the most precious. Gold is more precious than silver. |
| | 6. | Motorway, road, lane. A motorway is the widest. A road is wider than a lane. |
| | 7. | River, stream, puddle. A river is the deepest. A stream is deeper than a puddle. |
| | 8. | Plane, train, bicycle. A plane is the fastest. A train is faster than a bicycle. |
| | 9. | TV, cinema, theatre. TV is the most popular. The cinema is more popular than the theatre. |
| | 10. | Baby, infant, teenager. A baby is the youngest. An infant is younger than a teenager. |

## COMPARATIVE QUIZ – extension

**Comparative:** *City Z is larger than City Y.*
**Superlative:** *City X is the largest.*

Continue, as above, by getting the teams to write a number of similar problems for the other teams to solve. The problems could be about the country or area your course is taking place in, e.g. *City X, City Y, City Z* (large); *River A, River B, river C* (long); *Newspaper X, Newspaper Y, Newspaper Z* (big circulation). Check that the problems they write are not too difficult and that the team that has written the problem knows the answer. Also make sure there is no duplication of questions. Alternatively, prepare a number of problems yourself to put to the teams.

## COMPARISON GAME

**Comparative:** *Magazines are usually more expensive.*
*Magazines are usually thicker.*

Write up *Newspaper/Magazine*. Tell the class that they have to think of as many differences as they can between a newspaper and a magazine. Give some examples:

> *Magazines are usually more expensive.*
> *Magazines are usually thicker.*
> *Newspapers are generally more topical.*

then ask the class to think of some more differences.
Write up *Cinema/Theatre*. Divide the class into small teams of three to four players and appoint team secretaries. The team secretaries, helped by the rest of their team, have to write down as many differences as they can between the cinema and the theatre. Set a four-minute time limit. For example:

> *The cinema is generally more popular.*
> *Theatres are usually bigger.*
> *You generally have to book for the theatre.*
> *Cinemas are usually more comfortable.*
> *The theatre is usually more expensive.*
> *People dress up more to go to the theatre.*

The teams then read out their sentences. The team with the most sentences is the winner. Reject sentences if the class feels that any of the differences are not real ones. Continue the game with other comparisons. For example:

> *Travelling by train/car.*
> *TV in Country X/Country Y.*
> *Politicians/Business people.*
> *Indian/Chinese food.*
> *Football/American football.*
> *Holidays in Country X/Country Y.*
> *People from X/People from Y.*

# COMPARATIVE QUIZ

Put these words in the correct order and write sentences with the superlative and comparative.

**1. LARGE**

sea
ocean
lake

Ocean, sea, lake. An ocean is the largest. A sea is larger than a lake.

**2. IMPORTANT**

captain
sergeant
major

Major, captain, sergeant. A major is the most important. A captain is more important than a sergeant.

**3. BIG**

city
village
town

**4. STRONG**

whisky
beer
wine

**5. PRECIOUS**

gold
platinum
silver

**6. WIDE**

motorway
lane
road

**7. DEEP**

puddle
river
stream

**8. FAST**

train
plane
bicycle

**9. POPULAR**

cinema
TV
theatre

**10. YOUNG**

baby
teenager
infant

# MEMORY 3

**Present Perfect Simple:** *She's packed her suitcase.*
*He hasn't packed his suitcase.*

*Photocopy pages 33 and 89 to play this game.*

Divide the class into small teams of two or three players and appoint team secretaries. Hand out page 33 and give the teams two minutes to study and memorise the picture. The get the teams to cover or hand you back page 33. Hand out page 89 and go through the examples with the class. The team secretaries, helped by the rest of their team, write down what jobs the Wright family have and have not completed. They must not look back to the first page while doing this. The team with the most correct sentences is the winner.

| | | |
|---|---|---|
| ANSWERS: | 1. | She's packed her suitcase. |
| | 2. | She's made her bed. |
| | 3. | She hasn't switched off the lights. |
| | 4. | She's watered the plants. |
| | 5. | He hasn't packed his suitcase. |
| | 6. | He's picked up the car keys. |
| | 7. | He hasn't turned off the electric fire in the bathroom. |
| | 8. | He hasn't closed the windows. |
| | 9. | They haven't tidied their room. |
| | 10. | They've had a shower. |
| | 11. | They've washed their hair. |
| | 12. | They haven't taken the cat to the neighbour. |

## LONG SENTENCE GAME

**Present Perfect Simple:** *I've washed the dishes.*

Begin the game by saying *I've done a lot of jobs today. I've washed the dishes.* Explain that the first player has to repeat your sentence and then add something new, eg *I've washed the dishes and dried them.* The game continues with each player in turn trying to remember what the last player said and then adding something new to the list. Players get a minus point if they *(a)* make a memory mistake; or *(b)* hesitate too long. Do not give players minus points for grammar mistakes - just correct the mistake and allow the player to continue. Example round:

| | |
|---|---|
| Player 1: | *I've washed the dishes and dried them.* |
| Player 2: | *I've washed the dishes, dried them and put them away.* |
| Player 3: | *I've washed the dishes, dried them, put them away and cleaned the floor.* |
| Player 4: | *I've washed the dishes ...* (This player is gets a minus point because he or she can't remember what follows). |
| Player 5: | *I've washed the dishes, dried them, put them away, cleaned the floor and dusted the furniture.* |
| Player 6: | *I've washed the dishes ....* etc. |

And so on. You could then begin a new round with a different situation. For example: *He's done a lot of nice things this week. He's been to the cinema ... .* The player with the least number of minus points at the end of the game is the winner.

**Hints:** Play a trial round before playing properly.

## WHAT'S DIFFERENT?

**Present Perfect Simple:** *You've opened the matchbox.*

You need a number of objects for this game, e.g. *a matchbox, matches, a file, a piece of paper, a wastepaper bin, some scraps of old paper,* etc. Place the objects on and around a table or desk. Give the class one minute to study the objects. Then, without the class seeing, make a number of changes, e.g. *Put the matches into the matchbox, take a piece of paper out of the file, throw the scrap paper into the bin,* etc. The class then has to say what is different: *You've opened the matchbox. You've taken a piece of paper out of the file. You've thrown the paper into the bin.* You could then get the class to make changes for individual players to identify.

The Wright family are preparing to go away on holiday. What do they have to do before they leave?

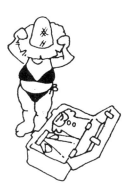

 1. Look at this picture for two minutes.

 2. Turn the page over.

 3. Then look at the second page.

© Colin Granger and John Plumb 1993

PHOTOCOPIABLE

# OBSERVATION 1

**Should:** *You shouldn't drive your car in the park.*

Divide the class into small teams of two to three players and appoint team secretaries. The first team to write the five *You shouldn't* sentences about the picture is the winner.

**Hints:** Afterwards, you could make sure that the class understands the information notices in the picture (*Boats £1 per hour* etc) as well as the prohibition notices (*Do not feed the ducks*, etc).

| ANSWERS: | You shouldn't play ball games/play with a ball. |
|---|---|
| | You shouldn't pick the flowers. |
| | You shouldn't walk on the grass. |
| | You shouldn't feed the ducks. |
| | You shouldn't fish in the lake. |

## WHERE IS IT?

**Should:** *You should hold the handrail.*
**Must:** *You mustn't stand too near the sides.*

Tell the class that you are going to describe a place. They have to guess where you are. For example:

> *In this place you should hold the handrail. You mustn't stand too near the sides.*
> *You mustn't take prams. You should carry young children and dogs.*
> *You should be careful when you come to the end ...*

Tell the class to say where you are as soon as they know, and not wait until you come to the end of your description. If they can't guess, give the solution: *On an escalator.* Working either individually or in pairs, get the players to write their own descriptions using *You should ..., You shouldn't ..., You must ...* and *You mustn't ...* sentences. If necessary, suggest some ideas (e.g. *in a library, on a plane, in a classroom, in hospital, in church, in a swimming-pool*). The players then read out their descriptions for the rest of the class to guess. You could award points to the player who is first to shout out the correct solution. Points could be deducted if players make a wrong guess while the description is still being read out.

# oBSERVATION 1

Six people in this park are doing something wrong. The park keeper is going to tell them off. What does he say?

*You shouldn't drive your car in the park.*

Find five more people who are doing something wrong and write what the park keeper says to them.

© Colin Granger and John Plumb 1993

# CONNECTIONS 2

**Infinitive of Purpose:** *I went to the estate agent to look for a house.*

The players must first match each object with a building (e.g. *the book with the library*), and then write a sentence for each pair, using the infinitive of purpose (e.g. *I went to the library to borrow a book.*) Set a ten to fifteen-minute time limit. The player with the most correct sentences is the winner.

| | | |
|---|---|---|
| ANSWERS: | 1 – F | I went to the estate agent to look for a house. |
| | 2 – A | I went to the restaurant to have a meal/dinner. |
| | 3 – B | I went to the library to borrow a book. |
| | 4 – D | I went to the travel agent to book a holiday. |
| | 5 – G | I went to the cinema to see a film. |
| | 6 – E | I went to the bank to cash a cheque. |
| | 7 – C | I went to the post office to post a parcel. |
| | 8 – H | I went to the station to catch a train. |

## INVENTION GAME

**Infinitive of Purpose:** *I went to the bank to change some money.*

Divide the class into small teams of two or three players and appoint team secretaries. Write up the basic structure *I went to the bank to ... .* Explain that the teams have to write as many structures as they can using that basic structure plus a clause containing an infinitive of purpose. The sentences have to be plausible (i.e. actions appropriate in a bank). For example, the teams could write:

*I went to the bank ...*   to change some Swiss francs.
to cash a cheque.
to put in some money.
to rob it.
to talk to the bank manager.
to get some change.
to change some traveller's cheques.

The teams must **not** just swop vocabulary while using the same verb (e.g. *I went to the bank to change some dollars. I went to the bank to change some marks. I went to the bank to change some lire.*). Set a three-minute time limit. Then get the teams to read out their sentences in turn. As the other teams read out their answers, the team secretaries should cross out any sentences on their list which are the same. At the end, the team with the most sentences left is the winner. (Check that all the sentences are appropriate.)
You could then play further rounds with different basic structures, for example:

*I telephoned the airport to ...*
*I went to the post office to ...*
*I stayed in the kitchen to ...*

# CONNECTIONS 2

Why did you go to these places? Find the matching pictures.
Then write a sentence.

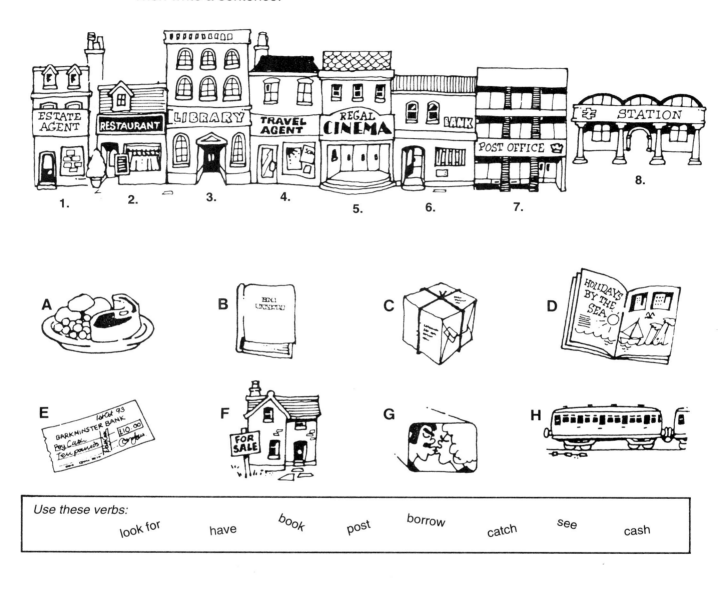

Use these verbs: look for, have, book, post, borrow, catch, see, cash

1–F  I went to the estate agent to look for a house.

# MEMORY 4

**Past Continuous:** *I was standing at the front of the queue.*

*Photocopy pages 39 and 90 to play this game.*

Divide the class into small teams of two to three players and appoint team secretaries. Hand out page 39 and give the teams two minutes to study and memorise the picture. Then get the teams to cover or hand you back page 39. Hand out page 90 and go through the examples with the class. The team secretaries helped by the rest of their team, write the answers to the questions on page 90. They must not look back the the first page while doing this. The team with the most correct answers is the winner.

| ANSWERS: | | |
|---|---|---|
| | 1. | I was standing near the front of the queue. |
| | 2. | A woman was standing behind me. |
| | 3. | She was wearing a dress. |
| | 4. | She was holding an envelope. |
| | 5. | The customer was sending a parcel. |
| | 6. | He was wearing jeans and a shirt. |
| | 7. | The clerk was giving him some stamps. |
| | 8. | The two men were carrying a bag. |
| | 9. | They were looking at the postman. |
| | 10. | The postman was unlocking the postbox. |

## PRIVATE EYE

**Past Continuous:** *What were you wearing?*
*I was wearing a suit.*

You need two large pictures or wallcharts showing a number of people in two different situations, for example, *In a shop, At the railway station*. The two pictures should be of approximately the same complexity and detail. Divide the class into two teams (Team A and Team B) and appoint team secretaries. Each team takes one of the pictures and chooses one of the people in it to identify with. Give the teams two minutes to memorise the situation of their picture. The two teams then exchange pictures and the team secretaries, helped by the rest of their team, write eight questions about the character the other team has chosen in their picture using the past continuous. For example:

*What were you wearing?*
*Who was standing next to you?*
*What was the woman standing next to you doing?*
*Who was coming in the door?*

Check that the questions are correctly expressed and use the past continuous. Team A then asks Team B their first question about Team B's picture. (Team B must not be able to see their picture at this stage.) One player from Team B, after a team consultation, answers the question. The players could take it in turns to answer questions. Score 2 points if the answer is both grammatically and factually correct; 1 point if only factually correct. Write up the score. Team B then asks their first question to Team A about Team A's picture, and so on, with the other 14 questions. At the end, the team with the most points is the winner.

## DETECTIVE STORY: 'SURPRISE THANK YOU'

**Past Continuous:** *Were they quarrelling?*
**Past Simple:** *Did the barman know the man?*

Read the story to the class, explaining any difficult vocabulary. Explain that the class must play detectives and find an explanation for the strange events in the story.

**The story**

*A man runs into a bar and asks the barman for a glass of water. The barman pulls out a gun and points it at the man. The man smiles and says 'Thank you'.*

The class then asks you questions to find an explanation for the story. They can only ask questions which have *Yes/No* answers, e.g. *Were they quarrelling? Did the barman know the man?* Give hints to elicit questions, e.g. *Ask me questions about what the man was doing when he ran into the bar. Ask me questions about why the barman pulled out the gun.*

**The solution**

*The man couldn't stop hiccuping. He ran into the bar to get a glass of water. The barman noticed that the man was hiccuping so he pulled out the gun and pointed it at the man to try to cure him by surprising him. The man was so scared that he stopped hiccuping and thanked the barman.*

You were standing in a post office when a robbery took place. The police are going to ask you some questions about what you saw. See how much you can remember.

 1. Look at the picture for two minutes.

 2. Turn the page over.

 3. Answer the questions on the second page.

© Colin Granger and John Plumb 1993

# BY WHOM?

**Passive (*was done*):** *'Yesterday' was sung by the Beatles.*

Divide the class into two teams, A and B, and appoint team secretaries. Team A asks Team B a question about picture 2. *Who invented the safety razor?* Team B can consult before answering. *The safety razor was invented by King Camp Gillette.* Team B then asks Team A a question about picture 3, and so on, with the other four questions. Score 1 point for each correct answer. At the end the team with the most points is the winner.

**Hints:** You could extend this quiz by asking the two teams to think of further questions beginning: *Who sung…? Who invented…? Who designed…? Who discovered…? Who wrote…? Who composed…? Who made…?*

ANSWERS:
1. 'Yesterday' was sung by the Beatles.
2. The safety razor was invented by King Camp Gillette.
3. St. Paul's Cathedral was designed by Sir Christopher Wren.
4. Penicillin was discovered by Alexander Fleming.
5. 'A Farewell to Arms' was written by Ernest Hemingway.
6. 'Porgy and Bess' was composed by George Gershwin.
7. 'Psycho' was made by Alfred Hitchcock.

## FAMOUS PLACES QUIZ

**Passive (*was done*):** *Napoleon was exiled on Elba.*

Prepare a list of famous places and a list of people or events which are associated with the places. Divide the class into two teams and appoint team secretaries. Explain to the two teams that you are going to write up a list of places and another list of people or events associated with them. The team secretaries, with the help of the rest of their team, should try to link a place with a person or event and write a sentence saying what happened there. Write up the two lists (in jumbled order) and give an example of the kind of sentence the teams are expected to produce, e.g. *Napoleon was exiled on Elba.*
Example lists: (Adapt to the knowledge of your class.)

**Places:** *Elba, Groote Schuur Hospital in South Africa, Bikini Atoll in the Pacific Ocean, Watergate Building in Washington, Dallas in Texas.*

**People/Events:** *Napoleon, the first heart transplant, the first hydrogen bomb test, the Democratic Party H.Q., President Kennedy.*

ANSWERS:
Napoleon was exiled on Elba.
The first heart transplant operation was performed in the Groote Schuur Hospital, South Africa (by Professor Christiaan Barnard).
Five men were caught bugging the Democratic Party H.Q. in the Watergate Building, Washington.
President Kennedy was assassinated in Dallas, Texas.

# BY WHOM?

Write a sentence about each picture.

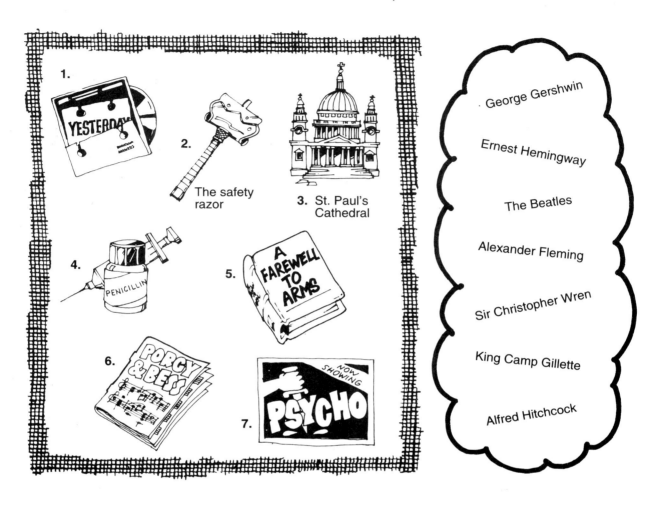

1.
2. The safety razor
3. St. Paul's Cathedral
4.
5.
6.
7.

George Gershwin

Ernest Hemingway

The Beatles

Alexander Fleming

Sir Christopher Wren

King Camp Gillette

Alfred Hitchcock

Use these verbs:

sing    make    discover    invent    write    design    compose

1. 'Yesterday' was sung by the Beatles.
2.
3.
4.
5.
6.
7.

© Colin Granger and John Plumb 1993

# SPOT THE DIFFERENCE 3

**Present Perfect + Yet:** *He has washed the tea towels.*
*He hasn't done the washing up yet.*

Working individually or in pairs, the players write down the jobs Frank has done and the jobs which still need to be done in picture B. Set a ten-minute time limit. The player with the most correct sentences is the winner.

| ANSWERS: | He has washed the tea towels. | He hasn't done the washing up yet. |
|---|---|---|
| | He has hung up his jacket | He hasn't cleaned the stove yet. |
| | He has vacuumed the floor. | He hasn't emptied the rubbish bin yet. |
| | He has done the ironing. | He hasn't swept the stair (carpet) yet. |
| | He has put away the dishes. | He hasn't cleared the table yet. |

## INVENTION GAME

**Present Perfect:** *I've read the dialogue.*

Divide the class into small teams of two to three players and appoint team secretaries. Write up the basic sentence *I've ... the dialogue.* Explain that the teams have to write as many sentences as they can using this basic structure with different past participles. The sentences have to be plausible (i.e the verbs must be appropriate to the rest of the sentence). For example the teams could write:

*I've* read *the dialogue. I've* written *the dialogue. I've* listened to *the dialogue.*
*I've* looked at *the dialogue. I've* learnt *the dialogue. I've* seen *the dialogue.*

Set a three-minute time limit. Then get the teams to read out their sentences in turn. As the other teams read out their answers, the team secretaries should cross out any sentences on their list which are the same as the ones read out. At the end, the team with the most sentences left is the winner. (Check that all the sentences are appropriate.)
Play further rounds with different basic sentences, for example:

*She's ... her boyfriend. We've ... the baby. He's ... a lot of money.*
*They've ... the washing machine. I've ... the house.*

## ACTION GAME

**Going to Future:** *You're going to open the door.*
**Present Continuous:** *You're opening the door.*
**Present Perfect + Just:** *You've just opened the door.*

Tell the class that you are going to act out various actions: some of the actions will be going to happen, some will be happening now and others will have just happened. The players have to tell you what the actions is, using: *You're going to ..., You're ...ing,* or *You've just ... .* Act out being about to open the door and point to the first player who has to immediately say *You're going to open the door.* Begin opening the door, and point to the second player who says *You're opening the door.* Point to the open door and to the third player who says *You've just opened the door.* The game continues in this way, like a chain drill, around the class. Players get minus points if they (a) don't respond with the correct statements; or (b) hesitate too long. Example round:

| Go to open the door | Player 1: | *You're going to open the door.* |
|---|---|---|
| Begin opening the door | Player 2: | *You're opening the door.* |
| Point to the open door | Player 3: | *You've just opened the door.* |
| Go to take out the cassette | Player 4: | *You're taking out the cassette.* |
| | | (This player gets a minus point for using the wrong tense.) |
| | Player 5: | *You're going to take out the cassette.* |
| Take out the cassette | Player 6: | *You're taking out the cassette.* |

And so on. The player with the least number of minus points at the end of the game is the winner. Example sequences of actions: *going to sit down, sitting down, have sat down; going to switch on the cassette player, switching on the cassette player, have switched on the cassette player; going to go out of the room, going out of the room, have gone out of the room; going to read, reading, have read.*
**Hints:** Play a trial round first.

# Spot the Difference 3

Frank does the housework every Saturday morning. In picture A, Frank is just starting to tidy up the kitchen. Picture B shows Frank still hard at work one hour later. What jobs has Frank done and what jobs hasn't he done yet in picture B?

Use these verbs:

put away    hang up
empty       iron
vacuum      clean
sweep       clear

*He has washed the tea towels.*
*He hasn't done the washing up yet.*

Find four more jobs Frank has done and four more jobs he hasn't done yet.

© Colin Granger and John Plumb 1993

PHOTOCOPIABLE

# MEMORY 5

***Anybody/Anything/Anywhere***: *Was there anybody choosing a book?*
*Was there anything written on the blackboard?*
*Was there a clock anywhere in the classroom?*

***Photocopy pages 45 and 91 to play this game.***

Divide the class into small teams of two to three players and appoint team secretaries. Hand out page 45 and give the teams two minutes to study and memorise the picture. The get the teams to cover or hand you back page 45. Hand out page 91 and go through the examples with the class. The team secretaries, helped by the rest of their team, write down the answers to the questions on page 91. They must not look back at the first page while doing this. The team with the most correct answers is the winner.

| ANSWERS: | 1. Yes | 4. Yes | 7. Yes |
|---|---|---|---|
| | 2. No | 5. No | 8. No |
| | 3. Yes | 6. No | 9. Yes |

## MEMORY 5 – extension

***Anybody/Anything/Anywhere***: *Is there anybody in the room wearing a blue shirt?*
*Is there anything on the floor near the door?*
*Is there an umbrella anywhere in the room?*

Tell the class that you have an excellent memory and that in a moment they are going to have an opportunity to test how good it is. Write up examples of the kind of questions they should ask you:

*Is there anything on the floor near the door?*
*Is there anybody in the room wearing a blue shirt?*
*Is there an umbrella anywhere in the room?*

Tell them that they should include questions which require a negative as well as a positive answer. Give yourself thirty seconds to study the room, its occupants, and everything which is in the room. Get somebody to time you while you do this. When the thirty seconds are up, tell the class to ask you questions to test your memory. Then sit in such a way that you can't see the room, and answer the class's questions.

***Hints:*** You could extend this game into a team game for two teams by taking in two large pictures or wallcharts of roughly equal complexity showing two different scenes involving a number of characters. The two teams have two minutes to memorise one of the situations. They then take it in turns to ask the other team *Is there anybody ...? Is there anything ...? Is there/Are there ... anywhere?* questions about the other team's picture.
Score 1 point for each correct response.

Look at this picture of a classroom in a Language School.

You have two minutes to try to memorise the situation.

# SPELLING QUIZ
**Vocabulary; Adjectives; Plural Nouns**

Working individually or in pairs, the players complete the quiz. The player with the most correct answers is the winner.

**Hints:** You could follow up the various sections of the quiz by, for example:

**Endings:** Get the players to think of a sentence using each adjective.

**Plurals:** With the help of the class, formulate spelling rules for plural nouns, e.g. *Nouns ending in* **f** *change to* **ves** *in the plural.*

**Differences:** Make sure the players know the meaning of the word which is not illustrated.

**Double letters:** With the help of the class, formulate rules for the doubling up of the final consonant in verbs, e.g. *In one syllable verbs ending in a vowel + consonant, the final consonant is doubled.*

---

ANSWERS:

**Endings**

| -able | -ible | -ous | -ful | -ive |
|---|---|---|---|---|
| excitable | sensible | courageous | careful | attractive |
| comfortable | horrible | poisonous | beautiful | expensive |
| agreeable | terrible | famous | truthful | possessive |

**Plurals**
thieves, fish, children, potatoes, glasses, bushes, boxes knives, babies, women, mice, feet, teeth, sheep, toys

**Differences**
1. scent
2. poor
3. mail
4. cereal
5. miner
6. heel
7. peace
8. stationery
9. brake

**Double letters**
1. He's cutting the grass.
2. She's knitting a scarf.
3. He's digging the garden.
4. He's travelling to London.
5. He's stopping the car.
6. She's beginning a letter.

---

## TOP AND TAILS
**Spelling; Vocabulary**

Divide the class into two teams, A and B. You could use a tennis metaphor to explain this game. Team A **serves** a word to Team B who have to **return** the serve by hitting back another word beginning with the last letter of Team A's word. Team A then have to hit it back by thinking of a word beginning with the last letter of Team B's word, and so on, until one of the teams loses a point by *(a)* hesitating too long; *(b)* not being able to think of a word beginning with the last letter of the previous word; or *(c)* making a spelling mistake thinking the last word ended in a different letter from which it does. Award 1 point to the other team whenever a team makes a mistake. Write up the score. Example round:

| | |
|---|---|
| Team A: | (serves) *Alarm.* |
| Team B: | *Meal.* |
| Team A: | *Lead.* |
| Team B: | ... (Team B hesitates too long - award 1 point to team A.) |
| Team B: | (serves) *Rail.* |
| Team A: | *Lovely.* |
| Team B: | *End.* (Team B makes a spelling mistake - award 1 point to team A.) |
| Team A: | (serves) *Plastic.* |
| | etc. |

Play until a team reaches a set number of points (e.g. 10 points).

**Hints:** Play this game at speed.

An alternative way of scoring would be to use the tennis system of *15-love (0), 30-love (0),* etc.

# Spelling Quiz

## Endings
Make an adjective from these words by adding an ending. Take care when you do this as sometimes you will have to change the spelling.
*For example:* exci<u>te</u> + able = excitable

fame, poison, attract, excite, possess, care, courage, sense, agree, truth, expense, beauty, horror, terror, comfort

-able
*excitable*
..................
..................

-ible
..................
..................

-ous
..................
..................

-ful
..................
..................

-ive
..................
..................

## Differences
These word pairs have the *same* sound but different meanings. Match the correct word in the pair with the picture.

toe/(tow)
1. sent/scent
2. pour/poor
3. mail/male
4. cereal/serial
5. minor/miner
6. heel/heal
7. peace/piece
8. stationary/stationery
9. break/brake

## Plurals
Write the plural of these words:

a thief — *thieves*
a fish
a child
a potato
a glass
a bush
a box
a knife
a baby
a woman
a mouse
a foot
a tooth
a sheep
a toy

## Double letters
Six of the verbs in the list below have double letters when you add -ing. Use these verbs to write about the pictures.

travel, stop, dig, work, hat, mow, begin, knit, cut, make, ride, write

1. He's cutting the grass.

© Colin Granger and John Plumb 1993

# CONNECTIONS 3

**Question Tags:** *Yes, isn't it?*
***So/Nor:*** *So do I./Nor can I.*

Divide the class into small teams of two to three players and appoint team secretaries. Set a time limit of three minutes for the team secretaries, helped by the rest of their team, to match the speakers. The team with the most correct answers is the winner.
***Hints:*** Afterwards, get the players to read out the conversations in pairs.

| ANSWERS: | A4 | B5 | C1 | D7 | E8 | F6 | G2 | H3 |
|---|---|---|---|---|---|---|---|---|

## AGREE OR DIE

***So/Nor:*** *So do I./Nor can I.*

Prepare a list of short statements for this game. For example:

> *I feel very well. I had a cold last week. But now I'm better. I can't complain. I've got enough money. I haven't got any debts. I'm not hungry. I'm sleeping well at night. Next week I'll get a raise. I can afford an occasional holiday. I went to the mountains last year. I didn't go skiing. I don't like winter sports. I'd rather go somewhere warm. I wouldn't like to live in a really cold climate. I might go to the South this summer. I couldn't go away last summer. I had too much work. I work in an office. My boss is very nice.* (So is mine.) *She isn't very old.* (Nor is mine.) *She's worked in the office since she left school. She's married. She hasn't got any children.*

Make sure your list has a good mix of tenses and auxiliary verbs. Explain to the class that they have to agree with the things you are going to tell them by using *So* or *Nor* responses. Tell the class that each player has two lives (three for a small class) and write up a *2* for each player as though you were writing up a class plan with students' names, For example:

```
                    22
           22              22
    22                           22
```

Change the plan whenever a player loses life, i.e. $2^1$. Players lose a life if they *(a)* make a grammatical mistake in their response; or *(b)* hesitate too long. Example round:

| You: | *I feel very well.* |
|---|---|
| Player 1: | *So do I.* |
| You: | *I had a cold last week.* |
| Player 2: | *So did I.* |
| You: | *But now I'm better.* |
| Player 3: | *So am I.* |
| You: | *I can't complain.* |
| Player 4: | *Nor can't I.* (Player 4 makes a mistake and so loses a life.) |
| You: | *I can't complain.* |
| Player 5: | *Nor can I.* |
| You: | *I've got enough money.* |
| Player 6: | *So have I.* |

And so on, with everybody, apart from Player 4, still with two lives. The last player left in is the winner.
***Hints:*** Play a trial round first.
AGREE OR DIE should be played at speed.
Involve players who are out in refereeing the game.

## SURPRISE

**Question Tags:** *You haven't, have you?*

Prepare a long list of 'surprising' statements, e.g. *I've been to prison. I robbed a bank. My brother's a murderer. My sister can't walk. I'm also very ill. I haven't got a penny. And I've got nowhere to live.* and play as AGREE OR DIE, but this time with the players having to show 'surprise'. For example:

| You: | *I've been in prison.* |
|---|---|
| Player 1: | *You haven't, have you?* |

# CONNECTIONS 3

Put the sentences below in pairs.

A – 4

## OBSERVATION 2

**Present Perfect Continuous:** *She has been pruning the tree.*

Divide the class into small teams of two to three players and appoint team secretaries. Set a time limit of five minutes for the team secretaries, helped by the rest of their team, to write down six more jobs Kate has been doing in the garden. The team with the most correct sentences is the winner.

**Hints:** After the class has completed this game you could ask them what evidence they found in the picture to base their observations on, for example, *There are some cut branches under the tree and a saw hanging on a branch.*

| ANSWERS: | She has been pruning the tree. |
|---|---|
| | She has been painting the fence. |
| | She has been watering the flowers. |
| | She has been cleaning the windows. |
| | She has been mending the gate. |
| | She has been burning rubbish. |
| | She has been cutting the grass. |

## SHERLOCK HOLMES

**Present Perfect Continuous:** *Have you been working?*

Explain to the class that you are going to mime an action and that they don't have to guess what action you are doing now but what action you have been doing. Mime walking along the road carrying two heavy shopping bags. (Your mime does not have to be good – the more amateur the mime, the more questions will have to be asked.) The class asks, *Have you been working?* (shake you head); *Have you been travelling on holiday?* (shake your head); *Have you been skiing?* (shake your head). Give verbal clues if necessary, e.g. *I'm in the city centre.* Continue until somebody asks *Have you been shopping?* The player who guesses the right answer then gets the chance to mime an action for the others to guess, and so on, until everyone has had a turn. Either let the players think of their own *has been doing* action or write an action on a slip of paper for them to mime. For example:

*limping home* (jogging);
*drying hair and body* (swimming);
*rubbing eyes and yawning* (studying);
*walking very suspiciously* (stealing);
*panting* (running).

# OBSERVATION 2

Kate has been doing a lot of work in her garden this afternoon.

*She has been pruning the tree.*

Find six more jobs she has been doing this afternoon.

| Use these verbs: | paint | water | clean | mend | burn | cut |
|---|---|---|---|---|---|---|

© Colin Granger and John Plumb 1993

# MEMORY 6

**Past Continuous:** *He was listening to the radio.*

*Photocopy pages 53 and 92 to play this game.*

Divide the class into small teams of two to three players and appoint team secretaries. Hand out page 53 and give the teams two minutes to study and memorise the picture. Then get the teams to cover or hand you back page 53. Hand out page 92 and go through the example with the class. The team secretaries, helped by the rest of their team, write what the people in the office were doing before their boss walked through the door. They must not look back at the first page while doing this. The team with the most correct sentences is the winner.

*Hints:* After the class has completed the game, get the players to say what the office workers are doing now their boss is in the office. For example:

1. *He's making a telephone call.*
2. *She's reading a report.*

| ANSWERS: | | |
|---|---|---|
| | 1. | He was listening to the radio. |
| | 2. | She was reading a magazine. |
| | 3. | She was cutting her nails. |
| | 4. | He was sleeping. |
| | 5. | She was doing a crossword puzzle. |
| | 6. | They were playing cards. |
| | 7. | They were looking at photographs (holiday photos). |

### DETECTIVE STORY: 'MURDER IN BROAD DAYLIGHT'

**Past Continuous:** *Were the two men walking on the same side of the street?*
**Past Simple:** *Did they know the woman?*

Read/act out the story to the class, explaining any difficult vocabulary. Explain that the class must play detectives and find an explanation for the strange events in the story.

**The story**
*Two men were walking down a street in the middle of a city. Suddenly one of them pulled out a revolver and shot a woman who was walking on the other side of the street. The police quickly came and arrested the man. Later in court the judge said to the man, 'This is a clear case of murder. There were many witnesses and the crime was committed in broad daylight. You are guilty of murder but I cannot send you to prison – you are free.'*

The class then asks you questions to try to find an explanation for the story. They can only ask questions which have *Yes/No* answers, e.g. *Were the two men walking on the same side of the street? Did they know the woman? Were the two men friends?* If necessary, give hints to elicit questions, e.g. *Ask me questions about the relationship between the two men. Ask me questions about how the two men were walking down the street. Ask me questions about who was in the courtroom.*

**The solution**
*The murderer didn't know the woman he murdered – it was a crime without a motive. The two men – the murderer and his brother – are Siamese twins. The judge had to let the murderer go free as otherwise it would have meant putting his innocent brother in prison with him.*

Everyone in the office thought their boss was out for the day when suddenly he opened the door...
Look at the picture of the office.

You have two minutes to try to memorise what everyone is doing.

# SPORTS QUIZ

**May:** *Each team may have up to eleven players ...*
**Should:** *One team should wear blue caps ...*
**Must:** *Players must not splash water ...*
**Can:** *The game can be played by two or four players.*

Working individually or in pairs, the players have to decide which set of rules goes with which sport. Set a ten-minute limit for this. The player who gets the most correct answers is the winner.

| ANSWERS: | A7 | B5 | C3 | D1 | E9 | F4 | G2 | H8 | I6 |

## SPORTS QUIZ – extension    *May; Should; Must; Can*

Ask the players to write one or two similar sets of rules of different sports or games for the rest of the class to guess. Check that the rules are not too difficult and that *may, should, must* and *can* are used correctly. Also make sure that there is no duplication of sports or games. The players then take it in turns to read out their rules for the class to guess which sport or game they belong to.

# Sports Quiz

Match the sport or game to the appropriate set of rules. Write the number of the sport or game in the correct box.

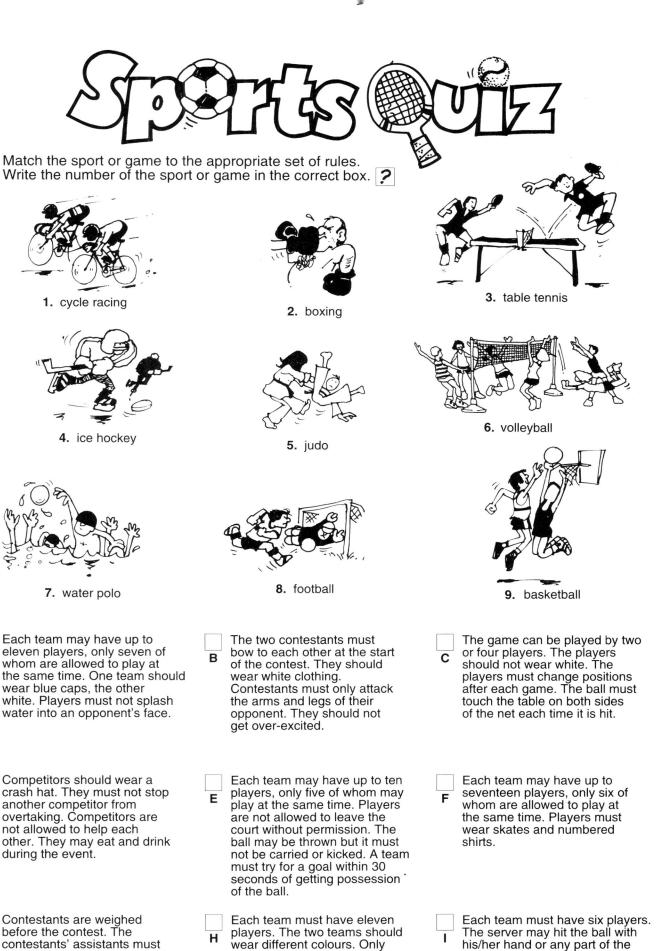

1. cycle racing
2. boxing
3. table tennis
4. ice hockey
5. judo
6. volleyball
7. water polo
8. football
9. basketball

A. Each team may have up to eleven players, only seven of whom are allowed to play at the same time. One team should wear blue caps, the other white. Players must not splash water into an opponent's face.

B. The two contestants must bow to each other at the start of the contest. They should wear white clothing. Contestants must only attack the arms and legs of their opponent. They should not get over-excited.

C. The game can be played by two or four players. The players should not wear white. The players must change positions after each game. The ball must touch the table on both sides of the net each time it is hit.

D. Competitors should wear a crash hat. They must not stop another competitor from overtaking. Competitors are not allowed to help each other. They may eat and drink during the event.

E. Each team may have up to ten players, only five of whom may play at the same time. Players are not allowed to leave the court without permission. The ball may be thrown but it must not be carried or kicked. A team must try for a goal within 30 seconds of getting possession of the ball.

F. Each team may have up to seventeen players, only six of whom are allowed to play at the same time. Players must wear skates and numbered shirts.

G. Contestants are weighed before the contest. The contestants' assistants must leave the ring before the fight begins. Contestants must wear gloves and must not hit an opponent behind the neck.

H. Each team must have eleven players. The two teams should wear different colours. Only the goalkeeper is allowed to play the ball with his/her hands or arms.

I. Each team must have six players. The server may hit the ball with his/her hand or any part of the arm. He/She must release the ball from his/her other hand before hitting it. Players must not touch the net.

© Colin Granger and John Plumb 1993

PHOTOCOPIABLE

# CLOSE-UPS 2

*Could be*: *It could be a watch.*

Working individually or in pairs, the players write sentences suggesting what objects the pictures show. The player with the most correct answers is the winner.

| ANSWERS: | 1. | It could be a watch. | 6. | It could be a wine glass. |
|---|---|---|---|---|
| | 2. | It could be a light bulb. | 7. | It could be a tap. |
| | 3. | It could be a penknife. | 8. | It could be a telephone. |
| | 4. | It could be a coin. | 9. | It could be a radio. |
| | 5. | It could be a (ball point) pen. | | |

## NOISES OFF

*Could be*: *It could be a pair of scissors.*

Some kind of screen is necessary for this game. You could construct one by putting two chairs on top of a table or desk and then covering them with a cloth or some coats. Take in some objects that make a recognisable sound when you use them, for example: *a pair of scissors, a retractable biro, a roll of sellotape, a zip, a book, a stapler, a date stamp, a newspaper, a clock, some matches and a match box, a lighter, a pencil sharpener.* Put the objects behind the screen, without the class seeing them. Ask for a volunteer to 'operate' the various objects behind the screen. The rest of the class, either as individual players or divided into two teams, have to guess what object they can hear by saying *It could be a ...* or, if they are very certain, *It's a ...* .

**Hints:** If you play this as a team game you could score: 1 point for a correct guess with *It could be a ...*; 2 points for a correct guess with *It's a ...*; but a penalty of minus 2 points for an incorrect guess with *It's a ...* .

You could play a variant of this game with smells (by taking in such things as *lavender, mint, garlic, coffee*); tastes (by taking in various food stuffs); and touch (by taking in various fabrics). In all these variants, the player in the guessing role would have to be blindfolded.

# CLOSE-UPS 2

Can you tell what these objects are?

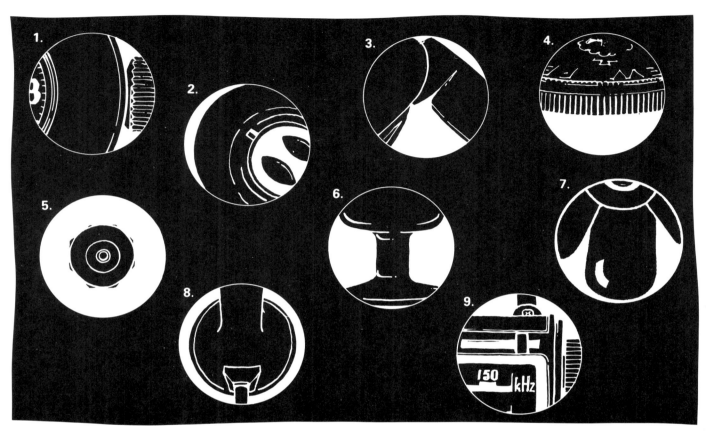

Use these words:

a telephone   a radio   a pen   a watch
a tap   a light bulb   a coin   a wine glass   a penknife

1. *It could be a watch.*
2. ......
3. ......
4. ......
5. ......
6. ......
7. ......
8. ......
9. ......

# CATEGORIES 2

***For/Since***: *for two days/since last night*

Working individually or in pairs, the players write the various time words and expressions under the appropriate column. The first player to correctly categorise the words is the winner.

| ANSWERS: | **for** | two days, five months, ages, a century, a few minutes, 30 years, ever, a moment, a long time, six hours. |
|---|---|---|
| | **since** | last night, lunch-time, yesterday, the Second World War, 12.30, September 1st, I was 20, last spring, Saturday night, 1950. |

## VOTING GAME

***For/Since***: *for quite a while/since midnight*

You will need a list of time words and expressions to play this game. Ask each player to write the words FOR and SINCE in large capital letters on separate pieces of paper. Explain that you are going to call out a number of time words and expressions and that after each one, the players should vote whether they would use *for* or *since* with that word or expression by holding up the appropriate piece of paper. They should vote in unison and not look at the others before deciding. Players get a minus point if they *(a)* hold up the wrong time word; or *(b)* hesitate too long. Begin to read out your list of time words and expressions, pausing after each one for the players to vote on which preposition to use. Example time words and expressions: *quite a while, midnight, two-fifteen, years, Easter, a few seconds, a while, last summer, 1900, three hours, last night, Tuesday morning, a lifetime.* The player with the least number of minus points is the winner.

**Hints:** Play a trial round first.

# CATEGORIES 2

Look at these time words and expressions. Some of them use 'for' and some use 'since'. Put them in the correct column.

12.30  lunch-time  yesterday  ages  the Second World War  a century
last night  two days  five months  a few minutes  a moment
Saturday night  six hours  last spring
a long time  1950  30 years  ever  September 1st  I was 20

| **for** | **since** |
|---|---|
| *two days* | *last night* |

# OBSERVATION 3

**Will (Predictions):** *Don't touch that wire. You'll get an electric shock.*

Divide the class into small teams of two to three players and appoint team secretaries. Set a ten-minute time limit for the team secretaries, helped by the rest of their team, to write the warnings. The team with the most correct questions is the winner.

| ANSWERS: | 1. | Don't touch that wire. You'll get an electric shock. |
|---|---|---|
| | 2. | Don't climb that tree. You'll fall. |
| | 3. | Don't sit on that bench. You'll get paint on your clothes. |
| | 4. | Don't play with that knife. You'll cut yourself. |
| | 5. | Don't lie in the sun. You'll get sunburnt. |
| | 6. | Don't go near that dog. You'll get bitten. |
| | 7. | Don't eat all those apples. You'll get stomachache. |
| | 8. | Don't swim in the river. You'll drown. |

## HELP!

**Will (Offers):** *I'll answer it.*

Prepare a list of prompts to elicit offers, for example, *Oh no! The phone's ringing. I'm thirsty.* Explain to the students that you are going to say something to them and they have to respond with an appropriate offer of help beginning with *I'll* … . Give one or two examples, e.g. *Oh no! The phone's ringing. – Don't worry, I'll answer it., I'm thirsty. – I'll get you a drink of water.* Then work around the class, giving individual students prompts. You could award points for each appropriate response. Example prompts:

*I'm hungry.*
*I've got a headache.*
*I've left my bag in the teachers' room.*
*It's very hot in this room.*
*Now it's a bit cold.*
*I'm still cold.*
*The board needs cleaning.*
*I haven't got a pen.*
*And I haven't got any paper.*
*I can't get the cassette recorder to work.*
*It's a bit dark in here.*
*I need a dictionary.*

# OBSERVATION 3

The eight people in the picture are about to do something dangerous.
Warn them not to do these things.

Use these words:

eat all those apples  touch that wire  swim in the river  get bitten  get paint on your clothes  drown  sit on that bench  go near that dog  get stomachache  cut yourself  play with that knife  lie in the sun  climb that tree  get an electric shock  fall  get sunburnt

1. Don't touch that wire. You'll get an electric shock.
2. 
3. 
4. 
5. 
6. 
7. 
8.

# MEMORY 7

**Used to:** *There used to be a post office.*
*There didn't use to be a supermarket.*

*Photocopy pages 63 and 93 to play this game.*

Divide the class into small teams of two to three players and appoint team secretaries. Hand out page 63 and give the teams two minutes to study and memorise the picture. Then get the teams to cover or hand you back page 63. Hand out page 93 and go through the examples with the class. The team secretaries, helped by the rest of their team, write down how the street has changed since the early 1950s. They must not look back at the first page while doing this. The team with the most correct sentences is the winner.

**Hints:** After completing the game you could ask the class to try to think of other possible changes in the street/town since the fifties. For example:

*There didn't use to be so much traffic.*
*There used to be more trees.*

| ANSWERS: | There used to be a greengrocer/butcher/newsagent.<br>There used to be a school.<br>There used to be a coffee bar.<br>There used to be a cinema.<br>There didn't use to be a car park.<br>There didn't use to be a bingo hall.<br>There didn't use to be a Chinese take-away.<br>There didn't use to be a post box. |
|---|---|

## THE GOOD OLD DAYS

**Used to:** *They used to salt it.*

Ask the class a number of questions about what man used to do before certain inventions existed. For example:

*How did people keep meat fresh before refrigeration was invented?*
*They used to salt it. (They used to smoke it.)*

Divide the class into two teams, A and B, and appoint team secretaries. The team secretaries, helped by the rest of their team, write a number of similar questions for the other team to solve. Check that the questions they write are not too difficult and that the team that has written the question knows the answer. also make sure there is no duplication of questions. Team A asks Team B their first question. Team B can consult together before answering. Help Team B with any difficult vocabulary – they only have to know the facts to answer correctly. Team B then ask Team A their first question, and so on with the teams' other questions. Score 1 point for each correct answer. At the end, the team with the most points is the winner. Example questions:

*How did people tell the time before clocks were invented?*
*How did people secure their doors before locks were invented?*
*How did people light their fires before matches were invented?*
*What did people cook on before gas and electric stoves were invented?*
*How did sailors navigate before compasses were invented?*
*What did people write on before paper was invented?*
*How did people produce books before the printing press was invented?*
*How did people exchange goods before money was invented?*

# The Good Old Days

This is what a typical street in Britain looked like in the early 1950s. Look at the picture. You have two minutes to try and remember what is in the street.

# THE WORD ORDER GAME

**Word Order**
**Adverbs of Frequency:** *He usually wakes up at half past seven.*

Divide the class into small teams of two to three players and appoint team secretaries. The team secretaries, helped by the rest of their team, have to write the six sentences in the three-minute time limit. The team with the most correct sentences is the winner.

| ANSWERS: | |
|---|---|
| 1. | I will meet you outside the cinema at quarter past seven/7.15. |
| 2. | She speaks Chinese very fluently. |
| 3. | Is your car faster than mine? |
| 4. | Do you often watch television? |
| 5. | There is not much typing paper in the drawer. |
| 6. | Could you pass me the salt? |

## *THE WORD ORDER GAME – extension*

**Word Order**
**Adverbs of Frequency:** *never, rarely, sometimes, often, usually, always*

Write up a list of the most important adverbs of frequency. Make sure everybody understands their meaning. Ask each team to agree on a sentence using one of these adverbs and to write out the sentence, putting each word on a separate piece of paper. Point out that the sentences should be of between eight and twelve words long, and that they could be questions or positive or negative statements. Remind them to write the question mark on a separate piece of paper if they choose to write a question. Each team then hands their sentence – in jumbled order – to another team to arrange into a sentence. Award points in terms of how many seconds, each team takes to do this. For example: *Team A 35 (seconds).* At the end, the team with the lowest total of points is the winner.

## *MAKE A SENTENCE*

**Word Order**

Write up a number *2 (3* for a very small class) for each player as though you were writing up a class plan with student's names. For example:

```
                22
        22              22
   22                        22
```

Explain that the *2* represents each player's 'lives'. The aim of the game is to make a grammatically correct sentence with each player in turn adding a word, e.g.

| Player 1: | *Why ...* |
| Player 2: | *Why can't ...* |
| Player 3: | *Why can't Susan ...* |

If a player thinks that it is impossible to continue the sentence, when it is his or her turn, he or she says, *Impossible.* This is a challenge to the preceding player. One of these players is going to lose a life. If the preceding player can add a grammatically correct word the player who challenges him or her loses a life, but the preceding player loses a life if he or she cannot do so. Players also lose a life if they add a word which is not grammatically correct. Example round:

| Player 1: | *Why ...* |
| Player 2: | *Why can't ...* |
| Player 3: | *Why can't Susan ...* |
| Player 4: | *Why can't Susan remember ...* |
| Player 5: | *Why can't Susan remember to ...* |
| Player 6: | *Why can't Susan remember to buying ...* |
| Player 7: | *Impossible!* (Player 7 thinks this is a grammatically incorrect sentence and challenges Player 6. Player 6 can't think of an end to this sentence and so loses a life. Cross out Player 6's 2 and write up 1). |
| Player 8: | (Player 8 begins a new sentence.) *Please ...* |
| Player 9: | *Please don't ...* |

And so on. The last player left is the winner.
**Hints:** Play a trial round before playing properly.
Involve the players who have lost both their lives in the scoring and refereeing.

# THE WORD ORDER GAME

You have three minutes to write six sentences.

_He usually wakes up at half past seven._

1.

2.

3.

4.

5.

6.

© Colin Granger and John Plumb 1993

PHOTOCOPIABLE

# OBSERVATION 4

**Present Perfect Continuous:** *Two children have been swimming.*

Divide the class into small teams of two to three players and appoint team secretaries. Give the teams ten to fifteen minutes to study the picture and for the team secretaries, helped by the rest of the players in their team, to write what the various people have been doing. The team with the most correct sentences is the winner.

**Hints:** You could get the teams to point out the 'evidence' for their statements, e.g. *Two people have been diving. They are carrying diving equipment. They are wearing swimming costumes. They are wet.*

| ANSWERS: | 1. These two children have been swimming. |
|---|---|
| | 2. This man has been walking. |
| | 3. These two men have been sightseeing. |
| | 4. This woman has been sunbathing. |
| | 5. This man has been playing tennis. |
| | 6. These two people have been diving. |
| | 7. This woman has been shopping. |
| | 8. This man has been painting. |

## LONG SENTENCE GAME

**Present Perfect Continuous:** *I've been sitting in the garden.*

Begin the game by saying *I've been sitting in the garden*. Explain that the first player has to repeat your sentence and then add another action he or she has been doing in the garden, e.g. *I've been sitting in the garden and I've been sunbathing*. The game continues with each player in turn trying to remember what the last player said and then adding something new to the list. Players get a minus point if they *(a)* make a memory mistake; *(b)* say an action which is inappropriate to the situation of *in the garden*; or *(c)* hesitate too long. Do not give players minus points for grammar mistakes – just correct the mistake and let the player continue. Example round:

Player 1: *I've been sitting in the garden and I've been sunbathing.*
Player 2: *I've been sitting in the garden, I've been sunbathing and I've been writing a letter.*
Player 3: *I've been sitting in the garden, I've been sunbathing, I've been writing a letter and I've been listening to the radio.*
Player 4: *I've been sitting in the garden, I've been ...* (This player hesitates too long and so gets a minus point).
Player 5: *I've been sitting in the garden, I've been sunbathing, I've been writing a letter, I've been listening to the radio and I've been humming.*
Player 6: *I've been sitting in the garden, I've been ...* etc.

And so on. You could then begin a new round with a different situation. For example:

*She's been typing letters in the office ...*

The player with the least number of minus points is the winner.
**Hints:** Play a trial round before playing properly.

# OBSERVATION 4

Look at this picture of the reception of a holiday hotel. You can tell what some of the people have been doing this morning by looking at the picture.

1. *These two children have been swimming.*

2. *This man has been walking.*

Write six more sentences using these verbs:

| swim | sightsee | sunbathe | play | dive | shop | paint | walk |

3. ....................................................................................................................

4. ....................................................................................................................

5. ....................................................................................................................

6. ....................................................................................................................

7. ....................................................................................................................

8. ....................................................................................................................

© Colin Granger and John Plumb 1993

# DEFINITIONS

**Relative Pronoun *(Who)* + Present Simple:** *A journalist is someone who writes for a newspaper.*

Divide the class into two teams (Team A and Team B) and appoint team secretaries. The team secretaries, helped by the rest of their team, write the definitions of the various jobs. The first team to complete this is the winner.

***Hints:*** You could extend this quiz by getting the two teams to write the names of eight more jobs for the other team to define. Check that the jobs they write are not too difficult and that there is no duplication of job titles.

| ANSWERS: | | |
|---|---|---|
| | 1. | A journalist is someone who writes for a newspaper. |
| | 2. | A mechanic is someone who repairs cars. |
| | 3. | A zoo keeper is someone who looks after animals. |
| | 4. | A greengrocer is someone who sells fruit and vegetables. |
| | 5. | A chef is someone who cooks in a restaurant. |
| | 6. | An optician is someone who tests people's eyes. |
| | 7. | A waiter is someone who serves food in a restaurant. |
| | 8. | An au pair is someone who looks after small children. |
| | 9. | A burglar is someone who steals from people's homes. |
| | 10. | A carpenter is someone who makes furniture out of wood. |

## CROSSWORD PUZZLES

**Relative Pronouns *(Who/Where/That)*:** *Someone who employs people. A place where you live. Something that you tidy your hair with.*

Write two crossword puzzles on different pieces of paper. For example:

**Crossword A**

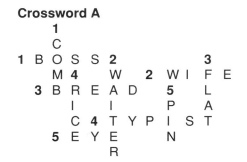

**Crossword B**

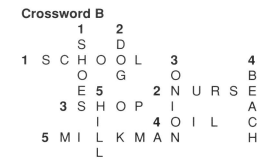

Divide the class into two teams (Team A and Team B) and appoint team secretaries. Give a crossword puzzle to each of the teams and explain that they have to write clues for their puzzle like this:

| 1 Down: | *Something that you tidy your hair with.* |
|---|---|
| 1 Across: | *Someone who employs people.* |
| 2 Down: | *Someone who works in a restaurant.* |
| 2 Across: | *Someone who has a husband.* |
| 3 Down: | *A place where you live.* |
| 3 Across: | *Something that you make sandwiches with.* |

When they have finished writing the clues, they should draw a frame for their crossword and give the clues and the frame to the other team for them to try to solve. Example frame for **Crossword A:**

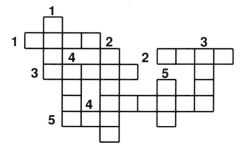

The two teams could then perhaps write and design their own crosswords for the other team to solve.

# DEFINITIONS

Find the correct definition for what these people do.

1. writes for a newspaper

2. repairs cars

3. looks after animals

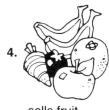
4. sells fruit and vegetables

5. cooks in a restaurant

6. tests people's eyes

7. serves food in a restaurant

8. looks after small children

9. steals from people's homes

10. makes furniture out of wood

*Use these words:* journalist, burglar, zoo keeper, waiter, greengrocer, au pair, optician, chef, mechanic, carpenter

1. A journalist is someone who writes for a newspaper.
2. 
3. 
4. 
5. 
6. 
7. 
8. 
9. 
10. 

© Colin Granger and John Plumb 1993

# MEMORY 8

**Lot of/Few/Little + Countable and Uncountable Nouns:** *There were a lot of eggs. There were only a few grapes. There was a lot of cheese. There was only a little butter.*

**Photocopy pages 71 and 94 to play this game.**

Divide the class into small teams of two to three players and appoint team secretaries. Hand out page 71 and give the teams two minutes to study and memorise the picture. Then get the teams to cover or hand you back page 71. Hand out page 94 and go through the examples with the class. The team secretaries, helped by the rest of their team, write sentences using the picture prompts on page 94. They must not look back to the first page while doing this. The team with the most correct answers is the winner.

| ANSWERS: | | | | |
|---|---|---|---|---|
| | 1. | There were a lot of eggs. | 7. | There was a lot of meat. |
| | 2. | There were only a few grapes. | 8. | There were only a few onions. |
| | 3. | There was a lot of cheese. | 9. | There were only a few tomatoes. |
| | 4. | There was only a little butter. | 10. | There was only a little oil. |
| | 5. | There was only a little milk. | 11. | There was a lot of orange juice. |
| | 6. | There were a lot of lemons. | 12. | There were a lot of sausages. |

## VOTING GAME

**Lot of + Countable and Uncountable Nouns:** *There were a lot of chairs. There was a lot of furniture.*

Ask each player to write in large letters *There were a lot of ...* and *There was a lot of...*, separately, on two sheets of paper. While they are doing this, prepare a list of countable and uncountable nouns. Explain that you are going to call out a number of nouns and that after each one, the players should 'vote' on whether the nouns are countable (*There were a lot of ...*) or uncountable (*There was a lot of ...*) by holding up the correct sheet of paper. They should 'vote' in unison and not look what the other players are doing before deciding. Players get a minus point if they *(a)* hold up the wrong card; or *(b)* hesitate too long. Begin to read out your list of nouns, pausing after each one for the players to 'vote' by holding up their sheets of paper. Example nouns: *chairs, furniture, rooms, space, people, hair, spaghetti, vegetables, children, money, notes, light, tea, cups of tea, happiness, examples, work, time, minutes, food, tins of food.* The player with the least number of minus points at the end is the winner.
**Hints:** Play a trial round before playing properly.

## LONG SENTENCE GAME

**Too Many/Too Much + Countable and Uncountable Nouns:** *At the party there were too many people and there was too much noise.*

Begin by saying, *At the party there were too many people*. Explain that the first player has to repeat your sentence and then add another complaint about the party, e.g. *At the party there were too many people and there was too much noise*. The game continues with each player in turn trying to remember what the last player said and then adding something new to the list. Players get a minus point if they *(a)* make a memory mistake; *(b)* say something which is inappropriate to the situation of *At the party*; or *(c)* hesitates too long. Do not give minus points for grammar mistakes – just correct the mistake and let the player continue. Example round:

| | |
|---|---|
| Player 1: | *At the party there were too many people and there was too much noise.* |
| Player 2: | *At the party there were too many people, there was too much noise and there was too much food.* |
| Player 3: | *At the party there were too many people, there was too much noise, there was too much food and there were too many men.* |
| Player 4: | *At the party there were too many people, there was too much noise, there was too much food, there were too many women ...* (This player makes a memory mistake and so gets a minus point.) |
| Player 5: | *At the party there were too many people, there was too much noise, there was too much food, there were too many men and there was too much light.* |
| Player 6: | *At the party there were too many people, there was ...* etc. |

And so on around the class. You could then begin a new round with a different situation. For example: *In the city there was ... .* The player who has the least number of minus points at the end is the winner.
**Hints:** Play a trial round before playing properly.

1. Look at the picture for two minutes.

2. Turn the page over.

3. Answer the question on the second page.

© Colin Granger and John Plumb 1993

PHOTOCOPIABLE

## OPPOSITES QUIZ

**Adjective (Prefixes):** *incorrect, uncomfortable, dishonest*

Working individually, or in pairs, the players write the opposites of the adjectives using one of the four prefixes. The first player to do this correctly is the winner.

| ANSWERS: | 1. incorrect | 5. inexpensive | 9. insufficient |
|---|---|---|---|
| | 2. uncomfortable | 6. unlucky | 10. impossible |
| | 3. dishonest | 7. impolite | 11. unfair |
| | 4. inaccurate | 8. dissatisfied | 12. impatient |

## VOTING GAME

**Adjective (Prefixes):** *mispronounce, impersonal, indirect*

You will need a list of adjectives and verbs which take prefixes to play this game. For example, *(mis)pronounce, (im)personal, (in)direct, (un)conscious, (dis)agreeable, (il)logical.* Ask each player to write *MIS-, IN-, UN-, DIS-, IL-* in large capital letters, separately, on six pieces of paper. Explain that you are going to call out a number of words and that after each one, the players should vote which prefix should be used by holding up the appropriate piece of paper. They should all vote in unison and not look at what the others are doing before deciding. Players get a minus point if they *(a)* hold up the wrong prefix; or *(b)* hesitate too long. Begin to read out your list of words, pausing after each one for the players to vote on which prefix to use. The player with the least number of minus points at the end is the winner.

*Hints:* Play a trial round first.

Example word list (adapt to the knowledge of your class):

**Mis** – pronounce, interpret, behave, understand, spell, calculate, represent
**Im** – personal, moral, proper, probably, mortal, perfect, plausible, practical
**In** – direct, dependent, complete, adequate, competent, efficient, experienced
**Un** – conscious, certain, equal, fashionable, fit, clean, aware, answered
**Dis** – agreeable, approve, organise, like, obey, pleased, content, believe, order
**Il** – logical, literate, legal, legible

# OPPOSITES QUIZ

Write the opposite of these words by adding these beginnings:

dis...   un...   im...   in...

1. correct
2. comfortable
3. honest
4. accurate
5. expensive
6. lucky
7. polite
8. satisfied
9. sufficient
10. possible
11. fair
12. patient

1. *incorrect*
2. ..........
3. ..........
4. ..........
5. ..........
6. ..........
7. ..........
8. ..........
9. ..........
10. ..........
11. ..........
12. ..........

© Colin Granger and John Plumb 1993

# WHERE?

**First Conditional (If + Will):** *If you go to Berlin, you'll see the Brandenburg Gate.*

Divide the class into two teams (Team A and Team B) and appoint team secretaries. The team secretaries, helped by the rest of their team, write seven *If you go, you'll see ...* sentences, joining the famous sights to the correct place names. The first team to complete this correctly is the winner.

**Hints:** You could extend this game by getting both teams to write five *If you go to + famous place ...* clauses and five *You'll see + famous sight* clauses. The five places shouldn't have anything to do with the five sights. For example one team might write:

*If you got to Pisa...; If you go to Athens...; If you go to the Louvre in Paris...; If you go to Rio...; If you go to Nepal...;*
*you'll see the White House; you'll see Mount Etna; you'll see the Pyramids; you'll see the Colosseum; you'll see the 'Bridge of Sighs'.*

Each team in turn then asks the other team to complete one of their half sentences, for example:

*If you go to Pisa, ... you'll see the Leaning Tower.*

Score one point per correct sentence. At the end, the team with the most points is the winner.

| ANSWERS: | |
|---|---|
| 1. | If you go to Berlin, you'll see the Brandenburg Gate. |
| 2. | If you go to Istanbul, you'll see St. Sophia. |
| 3. | If you go to New York, you'll see the Statue of Liberty. |
| 4. | If you go to Rome, you'll see the Colosseum. |
| 5. | If you go to London, you'll see Tower Bridge. |
| 6. | If you go to San Francisco, you'll see the Golden Gate Bridge. |
| 7. | If you go to Kyoto, you'll see the Golden Temple. |
| 8. | If you go to Paris, you'll see the Arc de Triomphe. |

## LOCAL KNOWLEDGE QUIZ

**First Conditional (If + Will/Might):** *How long will it take if I travel to Brighton by train? Who might you meet if you go to Buckingham Palace?*

Divide the class into two teams (Team A and Team B) and appoint team secretaries. The team secretaries, helped by the rest of their team, write eight questions about the local area. The questions should be in the first conditional. For example, if the local area is London, one team might write:

*Who might you meet if you go to Buckingham Palace? How long will it take if you travel to Brighton by train? What will you see if you go to Trafalgar Square? How much will you spend if you go to Green Park from here by Underground? What might you see if you go to Buckingham Palace? Why might you have to wait if you want to cross Tower Bridge? Which park will you see if you walk down Park Lane?*

Encourage the teams to write questions with different question words. Check that there is no duplication of questions and that the team that is to ask the question knows the answer. Check that the teams use *might* and *will* correctly. The teams then take it in turns to ask and answer these questions. Score one point for each correct answer. (In some cases approximate answers will do.) At the end, the team with the most points is the winner.

# WHERE?
## Famous Sights Quiz

*I want to go and see all these famous sights. Where will I have to go to see them?*

**1.** The Brandenburg Gate

**2.** St. Sophia

**3.** The Statue of Liberty

**4.** The Colosseum

**5.** Tower Bridge

**6.** The Golden Gate Bridge

**7.** The Golden Temple

**8.** The Arc de Triomphe

Use these words:
London    Kyoto    Berlin    Paris    Rome    San Francisco    New York    Istanbul

1. If you go to Berlin, you'll see the Brandenburg Gate.
2. ............................................................
3. ............................................................
4. ............................................................
5. ............................................................
6. ............................................................
7. ............................................................
8. ............................................................

© Colin Granger and John Plumb 1993

PHOTOCOPIABLE

# OBSERVATION 5

*Going to* **Future:** *A woman is going to dive into the water.*
**Present Perfect Simple + *Just*:** *A man has just dived into the water.*

Divide the class into small teams of two to three players and appoint team secretaries. The team secretaries, helped by the rest of their team, write four sentences describing what people are going to do, and four sentences describing what people have just done, in the picture. The first team to do this correctly is the winner.

**Hints:** You could get the team to point out the evidence for their statements, e.g. *a boy is going to buy an ice-cream – he's holding out some money and he's pointing to an ice-cream.*
*A man has just had a shower – he's coming out of the showers and he's wet.*

| ANSWERS: | A woman is going to get dressed. |
|---|---|
| | A boy is going to throw a ball. |
| | A boy is going to buy an ice-cream. |
| | A waiter is going to pour a drink. |
| | A boy has just eaten an ice-cream. |
| | A woman has just got out of the water. |
| | A man has just cut his finger. |
| | A man has just had a shower. |

## JUST DONE

**Present Perfect Simple + *Just*:** *Have you just had an accident?*

Prepare a number of slips of paper, each with a Present Perfect + *Just* sentence, e.g.

*I've just seen a ghost*  *I've just had a shower.*
*I've just lost my car keys.*  *I've just been to the dentist.*
*I've just been kissed.*  *I've just been told off.*
*I've just missed the bus.*  *I've just got up.*

Choose one of them and perform a suitable mime, e.g. *I've just seen a ghost,* mime *terror.* The class must then ask *Have you just...?* questions to elicit the correct *I've just ...* sentence. You answer by saying *Yes* or *No*, or by nodding or shaking your head. Give verbal clues, if necessary. Give the player who correctly guesses the sentence another sentence to mime for the rest of the class.

**Hints:** This game could also be played with Going to Future verbs, e.g. *I'm going to have an injection. It's going to rain. Somebody is going to hit me.*

## WHAT'S DIFFERENT?

**Present Perfect Simple + *Just*:** *You've just opened a drawer.*

Ask a player to look carefully at the room, and then to close his or her eyes for a moment. With the class's help, silently and quickly make five changes to objects and people in the room, e.g. *open a drawer, somebody takes off his jacket, two people change places, put a bag on a desk, write up something on the board.* The player then opens his or her eyes and has to say what is different: *You've just opened a drawer. You've just taken off your jacket,* etc. Score one point for each correct observation. Continue with each player in turn. At the end, the player with the most points is the winner.

# OBSERVATION 5

Look at this picture of a holiday hotel's swimming pool. Some people **are going to do** something, and some people **have just done** something.

A woman is going to dive into the water.

A man has just dived into the water.

Write four more **are going to do** sentences and
four more **have just done** sentences using these verbs:

| eat | cut | pour | get dressed | get out | buy | throw | have |

# CATEGORIES 3

**Phrasal Verbs:** *take off, look after, ring up*

Working individually or in pairs, the players have to complete the phrasal verbs by adding a preposition. The first player to do this correctly is the winner.

**Hints:** Get the players to put the phrasal verbs in a sentence when they have completed the game.
  For example: *He's just taken off his shirt.*
  *She's looking after my two children.*
  *I wonder who is ringing us up.*

| ANSWERS: | | | | | |
|---|---|---|---|---|---|
| | 1. take off | 4. take back | 7. knock out | 10. fill in | 13 put off |
| | 2. look after | 5. run over | 8. clear away | 11. look for | 14 get up |
| | 3. ring up | 6. listen to | 9. cut down | 12. try on | 15 keep out |

## STORYTELLING

**Phrasal Verbs:** *I woke up and put my hand out of bed.*

Begin the story by saying *I woke up*. Explain that the first player has to repeat your sentence and add something new to the story with a phrase or sentence including a phrasal verb, e.g. *I woke up and put my hand out of bed*. The game continues with each player in turn trying to remember what the last player said, and then adding something new to the story. Players get a minus point if they *(a)* make a memory mistake; *(b)* cannot think of a continuation to the story using a phrasal verb; or *(c)* hesitate too long. Do not give players minus points for grammar mistakes – just correct the mistake and allow the player to continue.

| | |
|---|---|
| Player 1: | *I woke up and put my hand out of bed.* |
| Player 2: | *I woke up, put my hand out of bed and picked up the alarm clock.* |
| Player 3: | *I woke up, put my hand out of bed and picked up the alarm clock. I looked at the clock in amazement.* |
| Player 4: | *I woke up, put my hand out of bed and picked up the alarm clock. I looked at the clock in amazement ...* (This player cannot think of a continuation to the story using a phrasal verb and so gets a minus point.) |
| Player 5: | *I woke up, put my hand out of bed and picked up the alarm clock. I looked at the clock in amazement. I turned the alarm off – it was eleven o'clock!* |
| Player 1: | *I woke up, put my hand out of bed and picked up the alarm clock. I looked at the clock in amazement. I turned the alarm off – it was eleven o'clock. I put the clock down.* |

And so on. The player with the least number of minus points at the end is the winner.

**Hints:** Play a trial round first.
  If your class find it difficult to think of phrasal verbs to continue the story give them mime prompts, e.g. mime *getting up, taking off pyjamas, putting on clothes, going to bathroom, switching on light, picking up toothpaste, taking off top, turning on tap, turning off tap, going downstairs, picking up newspaper, looking at headlines, putting cornflakes into bowl, sitting down, standing up.*
  You could play other games with starters such as:

*I walked down the street ...* (went into a stop, got on a bus, sat down, stood up, got off the bus, crossed over the road, looked into a shop window, etc.)

*I lay down on the beach ...* (put on my sunglasses, picked up a bottle, took off the cap, switched on the radio, etc.)

# CATEGORIES 3

Complete the phrasal verbs with these prepositions:

| off | after | to | for | out | on | back | away | in | up | over |
|---|---|---|---|---|---|---|---|---|---|---|
|   |   |   | down |   |   |   |   |   |   |   |

**1.** take off

**2.** look ......................

**3.** ring ......................

**4.** take ......................

**5.** run ......................

**6.** listen ......................

**7.** knock ......................

**8.** clear ......................

**9.** cut ......................

**10.** fill ......................

**11.** look ......................

**12.** try ......................

**13.** put ......................

**14.** get ......................

**15.** keep ......................

© Colin Granger and John Plumb 1993

PHOTOCOPIABLE

# BIRTHDAY QUIZ

**Second Conditional:** *I'd wear the cardigan*

Divide the class into small teams of two to three players and appoint team secretaries. The team secretaries, helped by the rest of their team, write eleven sentences about the birthday presents. The team with the most correct sentences is the winner.

**Hints:** You could extend this game by asking the teams what they would do with other presents. For example:

*What would you do if you got a necklace?* (I'd wear it.)
*What would you do if you got some fireworks?* (I'd light them.)
*What would you do if you got a pheasant?* (I'd eat it.)
*What would you do if you got a briefcase?* (I'd carry things in it.)
*What would you do if you got some binoculars?* (I'd look through them.)
*What would you do if you got a diary?* (I'd write in it.)
*What would you do if you got a pressure cooker?* (I'd cook with it.)
*What would you do if you got some stationery?* (I'd write on it.)

ANSWERS:
1. I'd wear the cardigan.
2. I'd read the recipe book.
3. I'd cash the cheque.
4. I'd eat the strawberries.
5. I'd cook with the herbs.
6. I'd sit on the cushion.
7. I'd spend the money.
8. I'd ride the scooter.
9. I'd plant the bulbs.
10. I'd hang up the poster.
11. I'd put on the perfume.
12. I'd play the drums.

# IMAGINE QUIZ

**Second Conditional:** *I'd be upset.*

You will need a list of situations for this game. (See example situations.) Divide the class into two teams, A and B, and appoint team secretaries. The team secretaries, helped by the rest of their team, write down what they and their team would do in the various situations. Introduce the first situation:

*Would you be pleased or upset if somebody said, 'You're so clumsy.'?*

Allow time for the players to consult together and for the team secretaries to write down *I'd be upset*. Then go onto the next situation:

*Would you be pleased or upset if somebody said to you, 'You're stunning.'?*

Continue with the other situations and then go through the situations once more getting the teams to tell you what their reactions would be. Score one point for each correct answer.
Example situations (Adapt to the knowledge of your class.):

*Would you be pleased or would you be upset if somebody said to you ... 'You're so clumsy/stunning/great/feeble/fascinating/embarrassing/thick/tedious/sentimental/witty.'?*

*Would you congratulate or feel sorry for somebody who told you ...*
*'I've come into a lot of money./I'm rushed off my feet./I got a raise./I'm worn out./I'm on the top of the world./I've been fired./I'm broke./I'm feeling a bit off colour at the moment./I've got pins and needles./I'm fit as a fiddle.'?*

# BIRTHDAY QUIZ

What would you do with these presents if you got them for your birthday?

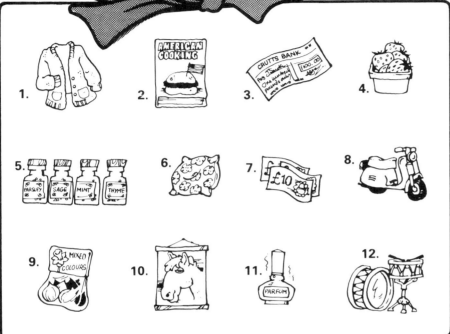

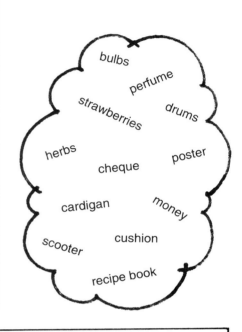

bulbs, perfume, strawberries, drums, herbs, poster, cheque, cardigan, money, scooter, cushion, recipe book

Use these verbs: wear, play, ride, hang up, eat, plant, read, sit on, cash, spend, cook with, put on

1. I'd wear the cardigan.
2. 
3. 
4. 
5. 
6. 
7. 
8. 
9. 
10. 
11. 
12. 

© Colin Granger and John Plumb 1993

# MEMORY 9

**Present Perfect Simple Passive:** *The picture has been taken off the wall.*

*Photocopy pages 83 and 95 to play this game.*

Divide the class into small teams of two or three players and appoint team secretaries. Hand out page 83 and give the teams two minutes to study the picture. Then get the teams to cover or hand you back page 83. Hand out page 95 and go through the example with the class. The team secretaries, helped by the rest of their team, should then write down what things are different. They must not look back at the first page while doing this. The team with the most correct sentences is the winner.

Alternatively, score two points if the sentences are both grammatically and factually correct, one point if only factually correct. The team with the most points is the winner.

| ANSWERS: | The ashtray has been used.<br>The drawer has been closed.<br>The wastepaper bin has been emptied.<br>The desk light has been turned on.<br>The computer has been turned off.<br>The blinds have been opened.<br>The cassette has been taken out of the tape recorder. |
|---|---|

## MEMORY 9 - extension

**Present Perfect Simple Passive:** *The lights have been switched on.*

Get two or three students to come out to the front of the class and look carefully at everything in the room. Then get them to leave the room for a moment while you – aided by the rest of the class – make five changes to objects in the room. For example: *switch on or off some of the lights, clean the board, unplug the cassette recorder, take a notice down from the wall, close a curtain or blind.* Then get the students to come back into the room and try to identify what five changes have been made. For example:

*The lights have been switched on. The board has been cleared. The cassette recorder has been unplugged. A notice has been taken down. The blind has been closed.*

Award one point for every change they notice. Continue playing the game, making different changes to the objects in the room every time a team leaves the room.

Look at this picture of a private detective's office. It's 7 o'clock at night and the detective is leaving. Look at all the objects in the room. You have two minutes to try and remember everything.

© Colin Granger and John Plumb 1993

# VOCABULARY QUIZ

**Vocabulary Revision**

Working individually or in pairs, the players complete the four sections of the vocabulary quiz. Set a five-minute time limit. Score one point for each correct answer. The player with the most points is the winner.

| ANSWERS: | **Odd Word Out** | |
| --- | --- | --- |
| | **Clothes** – docker  **Furniture** – boots  **Food** – spade  **Jobs** – spanner | |
| | **Opposites** | |
| | smooth/rough | soft/hard |
| | dark/light | sweet/sour |
| | ugly/beautiful | take off/put on |
| | tiny/huge | take down/hang up |
| | **Synonyms** | |
| | huge = enormous | rude = impolite |
| | ring up = telephone | tiny = minute |
| | icy = freezing | cheap = inexpensive |
| | pale = light | round = circular |
| | **Verbs** | |
| | sign a cheque | fold paper |
| | fill in a form | sew on a button |
| | splash water | polish shoes |
| | bounce a ball | hang up a coat |

## ABC GAME

**Vocabulary Revision**

Ask the first player to choose a category and announce it to the rest of the class (e.g. *animals*). This player then begins by saying the name of an animal beginning with the letter *A*. The next player has to follow by saying an animal beginning with *B*, and so on. Explain that all players have 3 lives and draw up a number class plan on the board, e.g.

```
                        33
               33              33
        33                            33
```

Players lose a life if they *(a)* cannot follow by naming a word within the category beginning with the next letter of the alphabet; *(b)* hesitate too long. When a player loses a life, the next player continues the game by announcing a new category and saying a word within that category beginning with the last letter. Example round:

| Player 1: | (announces the first category) *Animals.* |
| --- | --- |
| | *Adder.* |
| Player 2: | *Buffalo.* |
| Player 3: | *Camel.* |
| Player 4: | (This player hesitates too long and so loses a life.) |
| Player 5: | (announces a new category) *Places in Britain. Dover.* |
| Player 6: | *Edinburgh.* |

And so on, with everybody, apart from Player 4, still with 3 lives. The last player left in is the winner.

**Hints:** Make sure players do not choose categories which are too limited in scope.

Example categories: *furniture, countries, fruit and vegetables, clothes, parts of the body, food and drink, colours, jobs, things in a house, musical instruments, things in an office, tools, materials, things in a kitchen, means of transport, sports and hobbies, names of shops.*

Involve players who are out in scoring and refereeing the game.

# Vocabulary Quiz

## ODD WORD OUT

**Clothes**
cardigan
docker ✗
cap
scarf
vest

**Furniture**
stool
chest
wardrobe
desk
boots

**Food**
roll
pie
spinach
spade
fish

**Jobs**
printer
decorator
spanner
miner
surgeon

## OPPOSITES

Find the pairs of opposite words.

hard, put on, take down, dark, ugly, tiny, take off, smooth, sweet, rough, light, soft, beautiful, hang up, huge, sour

*smooth / rough*

## SYNONYMS

Find the words with the same meaning.

freezing, huge, ring up, icy, pale, rude, round, tiny, light, enormous, cheap, circular, minute, inexpensive, telephone, impolite

*huge = enormous*

## VERBS

Join one of these verbs to the most appropriate noun.

sew on, hang up, polish, fold, bounce, fill in, splash, sign, cheque, coat, form, shoes, water, paper, button, ball

*sign a cheque*

© Colin Granger and John Plumb 1993

PHOTOCOPIABLE

Now complete these sentences about the hospital. Don't look at the first page again until you have finished.

1. A porter is fetching *them a screen.*

5. A patient is lending ...........................................

2. The matron is giving ...........................................

6. A visitor is pouring ...........................................

3. A visitor is bringing ...........................................

7. A doctor is showing ...........................................

4. A nurse is passing ...........................................

Use these words: a screen, an injection, a thermometer, a glass of water, an X-ray, a pen, some flowers

© Colin Granger and John Plumb 1993

PHOTOCOPIABLE

ANSWER THESE QUESTIONS ABOUT THE HOTEL. DON'T LOOK AT THE FIRST PAGE UNTIL YOU HAVE FINISHED.

Put a tick ✓ in the correct box.

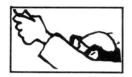

**1. What is his room number?**
- [ ] four hundred and two
- [ ] forty-two
- [ ] fourteen

**2. How many floors has the hotel got?**
- [ ] eight
- [ ] seven
- [ ] six

**3. Which floor does this guest want?**
- [ ] the fifth floor
- [ ] the second floor
- [ ] the fourth floor

**4. What time is it in the picture?**
- [ ] twelve fifteen
- [ ] twelve fifty-five
- [ ] twelve forty-five

**5. What date is it in the picure?**
- [ ] May the sixteenth
- [ ] May the sixth
- [ ] May the twenty-sixth

**6. How many people were arrested at the football match?**
- [ ] one hundred and ten
- [ ] one hundred and one
- [ ] one hundred

**7. What time can you have breakfast until?**
- [ ] half past eleven
- [ ] half past ten
- [ ] half past eight

**8. How much does a single bed cost per night?**
- [ ] thirty-two pounds
- [ ] twenty-five pounds
- [ ] twenty-three pounds

**9. Which bus are they waiting for?**
- [ ] seven
- [ ] seventeen
- [ ] seventy

© Colin Granger and John Plumb 1993

PHOTOCOPIABLE

# MEMORY 3

These are the jobs the Wrights have to do before they leave for their holiday. Try to remember if they have done the jobs or not.

1. Pack suitcase.
2. Make bed.
3. Switch off lights.
4. Water plants.

1. She's packed her suitcase.
2. ...................................................................
3. ...................................................................
4. ...................................................................

5. PACK SUITCASE.
6. PICK UP THE CAR KEYS.
7. TURN OFF ELECTRIC FIRE IN BATHROOM.
8. CLOSE WINDOWS.

5. ...................................................................
6. ...................................................................
7. ...................................................................
8. ...................................................................

9. Tidy room.
10. Have a shower.
11. Wash hair.
12. Take cat to neighbour.

9. ...................................................................
10. ..................................................................
11. ..................................................................
12. ..................................................................

© Colin Granger and John Plumb 1993

PHOTOCOPIABLE

1. **Where were you standing? (You)** (at the back, in the middle, near the front of the queue)

   I was standing near the front of the queue.

2. **Who was standing behind you?** (a woman, a man, a girl)

   A woman was standing behind me.

3. **What was the woman behind you wearing?** (skirt and pullover, a jacket and a skirt, a dress)

   ....................................................................................................................................

4. **What was she holding?** (a parcel, an envelope, a telegram)

   ....................................................................................................................................

5. **What was the customer at the front of the line sending?** (a telegram, a letter, a parcel)

   ....................................................................................................................................

6. **What was he wearing?** (a suit, jeans and a shirt, jeans and a jacket)

   ....................................................................................................................................

7. **What was the clerk giving him?** (some stamps, an envelope, a form)

   ....................................................................................................................................

8. **What were the two men coming into the post office carrying?** (a suitcase, a parcel, a bag)

   ....................................................................................................................................

9. **Who were they looking at?** (you, the postman, the clerk)

   ....................................................................................................................................

10. **What was the postman unlocking?** (the front door, the safe, the postbox)

    ....................................................................................................................................

© Colin Granger and John Plumb 1993

Put a ✓ in the correct box.

1. Was there anybody choosing a book?  YES ☐  NO ☐
2. Was there anybody looking at the classroom notice-board?  YES ☐  NO ☐
3. Was there anybody doing a test?  YES ☐  NO ☐
4. Was there anybody speaking to the teacher?  YES ☐  NO ☐
5. Was there anybody using the drinks machine?  YES ☐  NO ☐
6. Was there anything written on the blackboard?  YES ☐  NO ☐
7. Was there anything in the teacher's hands?  YES ☐  NO ☐
8. Was there a clock anywhere in the classroom?  YES ☐  NO ☐
9. Was there a cassette-player anywhere in the classroom?  YES ☐  NO ☐

ANSWER THESE QUESTIONS ABOUT THE LANGUAGE SCHOOL. DO NOT LOOK AT THE FIRST PAGE AGAIN UNTIL YOU HAVE FINISHED.

© Colin Granger and John Plumb 1993

PHOTOCOPIABLE

Write what all the people in the office were doing at the moment their boss opened the door. Do not look at the first page again until you have finished.

1. He was listening to the radio.
2.
3.
4.
5.
6.
7.

THIS IS WHAT THE STREET IS LIKE TODAY.

How has the street changed? Write sentences like these:

*There used to be a post office.*
*There didn't use to be a supermarket.*

Write four more **There used to be** and four more **There didn't use to be** sentences about the street. Do not look at the first page again until you have finished.

© Colin Granger and John Plumb 1993

Write sentences.

1.    2.    3.    4.

5.    6.    7.    8.

9.    10.    11.    12.

1. There were a lot of eggs.
2. There were only a few grapes.
3. There was a lot of cheese.
4. There was only a little butter.
5. 
6. 
7. 
8. 
9. 
10. 
11. 
12. 

© Colin Granger and John Plumb 1993

The photo has been taken off the wall.

**What are the other seven things?**

| Use these words: | close | take out | empty | use | turn on | turn off | open |

# INDEX OF STRUCTURE AND LANGUAGE POINTS

|  |  |  |
|---|---|---|
| A | There's *a* lipstick. | 10 |
| Adjectives | It's quite *big*, but it isn't very *heavy*. | 22,46 |
| (+ prefixes) | *in*correct, *un*comfortable, *dis*honest. | 72 |
| (comparatives + superlatives) | A sea is *larger than* a lake. An ocean is *the largest*. | 30 |
| Adverbs (frequency) | He *usually* wakes up at half-past seven. | 64 |
| (manner) | He drives very *dangerously*. | 26 |
| Any | There aren't *any* chips. | 10 |
| Anybody | Is there *anybody* choosing a book? | 44 |
| Anything | Was there *anything* written on the blackboard? | 44 |
| Anywhere | Is there an umbrella *anywhere*? | 44 |
| Articles (a) | There's *a* lipstick. | 10 |
| Be (verb *to be*) | It*'s* a cooker. They*'re* plates. | 8,22 |
| Can (possibility) | The game *can* be played by two or four players. | 54 |
| Comparatives (adjectives) | A sea is *larger than* a lake. | 30 |
| Conditional (first) | *If* you go to Berlin, *you'll see* the Brandenburg gate. | 74 |
| (second) | *I'd wear* the cardigan. | 80 |
| Could be (possibility) | It *could be* a watch. | 56 |
| Countable Nouns | There aren't any *chips*. | 11,70 |
| Dates | It's *May the sixth*. | 16 |
| Describing (people) | A journalist *is someone who* works for a newspaper. | 68 |
| (objects) | It i*s made of metal and plastic*. | 22 |
| Few | There were only a *few* grapes. | 70 |
| For | *for* two days. | 58 |
| Going to (future) | She*'s going to play* the piano. | 28,42,76 |
| If | *If* you go to Berlin, you'll see the Brandenburg gate. | 74 |
| Imperative | *Do not lean* out of the window. | 20,62 |
| Infinitive of Purpose | I went to the estate agent's *to look* for a house. | 36 |
| Just | A man has *just* dived into the water. | 42,76 |
| Little | There was only a *little* butter. | 70 |
| Lot of | There was a *lot of* cheese. | 70 |
| Many/Much | At the party there were too *many* people and there was too *much* noise. | 70 |
| May (permission) | Each team *may have* up to eleven players. | 54 |
| Might | Who *might* you meet if you go to Buckingham Palace? | 74 |
| Modal Verbs – see: | can, could, may, might, must, should | |
| Must, Mustn't (obligation) | Players *must not* splash water. | 54 |
| Nor | I can't swim. *Nor* can I. | 48 |
| Nouns (singular + plural) | It's a *cooker*. They're *plates*. There are some *envelopes*. | 8,10,46 |
| (countable/uncountable) | There is some *fruit salad*.There aren't any *chips*. | 10 |
| Numbers | *Four hundred and two*/t*he fifth* floor. | 16 |
| Passive (Present Simple) | It *is used* by photographers. | 22 |
| (Past) | 'Yesterday' *was sung* by the Beatles. | 40 |
| (Present Perfect) | The picture *has been taken* off the wall. | 82 |
| Past Continuous | *I was standing* near the front of the queue. | 38,52 |
| Past Simple | Last night, Frank *woke up*. | 24,38,52 |
| Phrasal Verbs | *Take off, look after, ring up* | 78 |
| Prepositions of Place | The towel should be *behind* the door. | 18 |
| Present Continuous | A porter *is fetching* them a screen. | 6 |
| Present Simple | Carpenters *make* things from wood. | 14,22,26,42,68 |
| Present Perfect | She*'s packed* her suitcase. | 32,42,76 |
| (vs.*going to*) | *is going to /has just done* | 76 |
| Present Perfect Continuous | She *has been pruning* the tree. | 50,66 |
| Pronouns (object) | A porter is fetching *them* a screen. | 6 |
| (relative) | A journalist is someone *who* writes for a newspaper. | 68 |
| Question Tags | You're not, *are you?* | 48 |
| Relative Pronouns | A journalist is someone *who* writes for a newspaper. | 68 |
| Should (obligation) | You *shouldn't drive* your car in the park. | 34,54 |
| Should be | The towel *should be* behind the door. | 18 |
| Since | *since* last night. | 58 |
| So (So do I) | I hate cold coffee. *So do I*. | 48 |
| Some | There is *some* fruit salad. | 10 |
| Spelling | | 46 |
| Superlatives | An ocean is *the largest*. | 30 |
| That | Something *that* you tidy your hair with. | 68 |
| There is/there are | *There is* some fruit salad. *There aren't* any chips. | 10,18 |
| This/these | What is *this*? What are *these*? | 8 |
| Time | *It's twelve forty-five*. | 16 |
| Too | There were *too* many people and there was *too* much noise. | 70 |
| Used to | There *used to* be a post office. | 62 |
| Uncountable nouns | The is some *fruit salad*. | 11,70 |
| Vocabulary | Food, clothes, parts of the body, transport, places, furniture. | 12,84 |
| Will (predictions) | You*'ll* get an electric shock. | 60 |
| (offers) | *I'll* answer it. | 60 |
| (conditional) | If you go to Berlin, you*'ll* see the Brandenburg gate. | 74 |
| Where (relative pronoun) | A place *where* you live. | 68 |
| Who (relative pronoun) | A journalist is someone *who* writes for a newspaper. | 68 |
| Word Order | He *usually* wakes up at half-past seven. | 64 |
| Would | *I'd wear* the cardigan. | 80 |
| Yet | He hasn't done the washing up *yet*. | 42 |